July 1985

D1296290

Alys B. Davis

DECORATIVE STUFFED TOYS
for the Needleworker

Instructions and Full-Size Patterns
for Embroidered Animals
Dolls and Ornaments

WINSOME DOUGLASS

DOVER PUBLICATIONS, INC.
New York

ACKNOWLEDGMENTS

The author and publishers acknowledge with gratitude the help of Needlework Development Scheme, Glasgow, in kindly making available the photographs reproduced in Plates 1, 2, 3, 4, 7 and 8. All the photographs were taken by Studio Swain of Glasgow.

Published in Canada by General Publishing Company, Ltd., 30 Lesmill Road, Don Mills, Toronto, Ontario.

This Dover edition, first published in 1984, is an unabridged republication of the work first published under the title *Toys for Your Delight* by Mills and Boon Limited, London, in 1957. The present edition is published by special arrangement with Bell & Hyman, Publishers, Denmark House, 37/39 Queen Elizabeth Street, London SE1 2QB. The three color plates (nos. 5 and 6 and frontispiece) appear in black and white in the Dover edition.

Manufactured in the United States of America
Dover Publications, Inc., 31 East 2nd Street, Mineola, N.Y. 11501

Library of Congress Cataloging in Publication Data

Douglass, Winsome.
  Decorative stuffed toys for the needleworker.

  Reprint. Originally published: Toys for your delight. London : Mills & Boon, 1957.
  Includes index.
  1. Soft toy making.   2. Embroidery.   I. Title.
  TT174.3.D67   1984   745.592'4   83-20601
  ISBN 0-486-24638-8

CONTENTS

LIST OF PLATES

Representing toys designed and worked by the author

Section One

INTRODUCTION

I NEVER THINK OF THE POEM by Robert Louis Stevenson which begins " I will make you brooches and toys for your delight " without conjuring in my mind's eye a wealth of wonderful and exciting playthings—toys that would delight the heart and mind of anyone, old or young. For toys can be the most inspiring things—especially to the creator. I suppose they will have been in existence since the beginning of time when man first fashioned creatures from clay as playthings for his children or as gifts to his mate. Toys such as rattles, whistles and very simple music-making instruments rank among the oldest of them. Then we have such playthings as hoops, spinning tops, balls and kites, not forgetting weapons like the bow and catapult.

Receptacles for carrying things were a kind of toy. They were fashioned from clay, straw, wicker work and wood. The wooden toys could be jointed. Others were fastened with thorns. Some toys originated as images or gods used for certain rituals. When the feast or ritual was over or when it had lost its significance through a change in the custom the images were retained as playthings or ornaments. Some images were endowed with magic properties and were used as charms. They were given to children to restore health or protect them from ailments. Often too they were given as parting gifts. Because of their fragility and the ephemeral character of many of the materials from which they were made, many ancient toys unfortunately have not survived the test of time.

I think perhaps a great deal of their charm lies in the fact that they are nearly always reproduced in miniature and one tends to lavish affection on something that is small. The girls would have small dolls and the boys small weapons in preparation for the time when they would be required to look after and use the real thing. So toys have their uses too ! But even when time was taken up with the important business of living and hunting the old affection for the playthings of childhood still lingered—as it does to-day. We all know the story of the untidy golliwog or teddy bear that brings back memories so vivid that it seems almost a sacrilege to part with such a dear old thing.

From the dolls and weapons I should imagine the next step would be to reproduce models of creatures that lived with you—animals, birds, reptiles, etc., perhaps as a progression from scratching their likenesses on cave walls and clay pots. How much more satisfying to see a creature actually in the round—one created by you—and what fun you could have making him fierce or gentle, swiftly galloping or curled asleep. You see, the creator of the toy has absolute control over it, or perhaps I should say almost absolute control, because sometimes the toys seem to take on a life of their own and all kinds of little twists and quirks develop as they are being fashioned. No doubt this kind of toy would become a decoration rather than a plaything, and has eventually deteriorated into the pot animals we so often see sitting in the windows—all alike, no different from the pot dog next door. What a pity! But the hand-made toy can have its own personality whether it be for a plaything or a decoration—that is the privilege of the creator. You can simplify or exaggerate any characteristic you choose; you can even make a wicked crocodile smile until he seems to be the gentlest pet on earth. You can create a savage brigand with a fearsome scowl who makes you tremble when you look at him, until you remember that he is only a doll after all and he is really very nice underneath his frightening exterior.

For toys are objects of affection. Just think—the oldest and staidest of us once played with toys. But even if the joy of playing with them is past, the joy of creation can remain. Bring to mind all the men who still play with model railways, build model ships and dolls' houses and really enjoy doing it.

Although many materials can be used for the making of toys—clay, wood, metal, plastics, etc.—I have chosen to deal in the main with those which can be stitched. Many women who do not usually care for sewing might enjoy making a simple toy from a given pattern, and it is only a short step from there to making your own patterns and creating your own creatures. You can make playthings for your children or grandchildren just as they would like them—give them all the charm and originality that is never found in the mass-produced article. I always think that if the creator has loved making her toy and lavished affection on it, the finished object retains that same love and charm for ever. Sometimes too, in some subtle way, these toys can give you a certain insight into the character of the maker. Very often when children first make a doll it turns out to look as they do themselves!

The patterns given in this book range from the very simplest to the more elaborate —but the reader must not stop at that. I hope she will go on creating her own designs and patterns and that this will only be the beginning. Most of the diagrams are actual size and patterns can be made from them by tracing, but they can quite easily be enlarged by squaring off the page and re-drawing the pattern on larger squares. As far as possible I have kept the simpler decoration for the simplest toys and have arranged the patterns so that they become progressively more difficult in their separate sections.

EQUIPMENT

The equipment necessary is not elaborate: a pair of cutting-out scissors, a small pair of sharply pointed scissors for clipping, several sizes of needle, both embroidery and sewing, a thimble—this is most important as it prevents stained work and damaged finger-ends—and a piece of smooth stick, long and with a tapered but rounded end for stuffing. A knitting needle which is not too sharp or a wooden meat skewer serves the purpose. It must be thin or you cannot reach the narrow parts of the animal when stuffing, but the point must not be too sharp or you will drive holes through the fabric when pushing in the stuffing.

MATERIALS

As for materials, a great variety may be used. In fact very often the creature itself suggests the fabric to you. For instance a rough woolly fabric may be suitable for a donkey, or a delicate organdie or nylon for a butterfly wing. Do consider and turn over in your mind the possibilities of different fabrics before starting on your toy. Even the feel of a piece of material may influence your final choice. Do not tie yourself to one material, experiment with various kinds and in no time at all you will find yourself evolving a most exciting creature. It is a good plan to keep a box or bag with all your scraps in it—ironed and flat so that you can see their colour and feel their textures easily. Keep everything—felt, cotton, silk, satin, wool, leather, fur, furcloth, towelling, nylon— anything which may be useful. In the main the larger pieces of fabric are best—I think it is a fallacy that toys can be made from small scraps. Some of the toy shapes are rather awkward to fit on to small pieces of fabric, especially when one must consider the grain of the material.

This last point is important and you must be careful to see that the pattern shapes are placed on the straight grain of the material, otherwise the stuffing will be difficult and the true shape of the creature lost.

One further piece of advice about cutting out—do be accurate, cutting right into corners and bends, especially if the toy is a small one, because even a fraction of an inch can make a difference to the finished article.

Felt of course is ideal for beginners—it has no edges to fray and no grain. One can cut exactly to the pattern without leaving turnings and one can place the shapes on the material at any angle. Young children find felt very easy to handle and it is wise to begin with it so that a large measure of success is assured.

After felt I think firm cotton fabric works up very well, and then firmly woven woollen materials. Silks, crêpe de Chine, satin, organdie and nylon need extremely careful handling and it would be wiser to experiment with the firmer fabrics first. If you are using a fabric with a pattern printed on it see that the scale of the design is suitable for the size of the animal ; very small animals will look better if the pattern on the material is also small—then one can appreciate both the shape of the toy and the design of the fabric. Too large a pattern results in perhaps only a small part of it being shown when the animal shape has been cut out. And often it does not fit in with the general design of the toy. After all, the decoration on the toy, whether it be in the fabric or applied afterwards, should be related to the general shape so that a pleasing and complete piece of craftsman-ship is the final result. One must be careful with fur or furry fabrics. If the pile is too long for the size of the toy the outline and shape are obscured, resulting in something that is clumsy and ungainly.

Many animals themselves suggest the kind of material most suitable—for instance furry cloth for a teddy bear, or smooth pink velveteen for a piglet. But one need not be hampered by adhering too closely to the most obvious ideas. I do advise the reader to try out other materials—those perhaps which do not leap to the mind immediately. Sometimes the idea will come when you are just turning over the scraps in your box. You will certainly find the making of the toy much more interesting and most likely will create a creature with vigour and individuality.

One need not stop at using the same fabric for the whole of the animal. Try com-bining two or more different ones—perhaps a plain and a patterned, or two different colours, or a spotted and a striped—the combinations are legion. It is advisable though, if you do this, to see that the several different materials are more or less of the same weight unless the parts of the creature are separate—such as a velvet body and organdie wings for an insect. Perhaps you could try the outside and back of a horse or deer in a dark colour, and the underbody in a light one, or one side of a creature dark with light decoration and the other side a counter-change. You could even divide up the creature and make a patchwork animal, the head, body, legs and undergusset all in different colours or fabrics. There is no end to the various ways in which one can assemble patterns and colours. Do choose your colour carefully, though. On the whole strong contrasts make for gay and sparkling effects, and remember that it is not necessary to have a great many colours for a lively finish. Too many strong colours just look jazzy and confused and detract from the shape of the toy. Tones can be as effective as contrasts, but as a rule produce a more subdued finish. For a beginner it is wise to limit your colours to three or four.

Most of the patterns I have included show simple shapes. Generally speaking if the main pattern shapes of the toy are complicated there is less scope for decoration, and the toy is difficult to assemble. A good thing to remember when you are making your own patterns is to keep the outline as simple as possible. This can quite easily be done without destroying the essential characteristics of the toy. Do not make legs and necks too thin, particularly if the toys are to be playthings for children. When drawing out your shape keep the legs thicker than you wish the finished ones to appear—some of the width will be taken up with the stuffing when the legs acquire a roundness.

DECORATION OF TOYS

All the toys illustrated have some kind of stitchery on them, but they can look attractive without any decoration, although even a little embroidery adds to their charm. I have included toys which have a design freely embroidered on them—the design fitting into the body or the neck or leg of the animal, but not related in any way to its coat texture or its markings.

Then we have designs built on the pattern of the fabric—perhaps elaborating a spotted material, either emphasizing the spots with stitching or joining them together in some way to form a design. Here again it is a good thing to keep the little designs within the shape of the body or head or whatever part of the creature you are decorating, and not let them trail off into something that looks unfinished. Sprigged, checked or striped fabrics are ideal for this method of decoration. Some ways of using patterned fabrics can be seen on page 5. Couching is a good method for elaborating a toy, especially when the background fabric is thick. The couched threads are wound or looped into interesting patterns and the stitching is simple. A thick thread couched with a fine thread requires little skill. This eliminates dragging thick needles through unwieldy material and prevents the pattern from being pulled out of shape.

Another method of decoration is appliqué. You can use this with felt without any fear of failure.

The simplest decoration is to cut small separate shapes such as spots or squares or triangles, and hem them into position with a matching thread. As you become more skilful you could vary the size of these shapes, making them fit into the appropriate place on the creature. They look better if you space them well and try them out before stitching

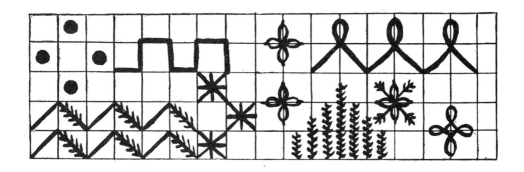

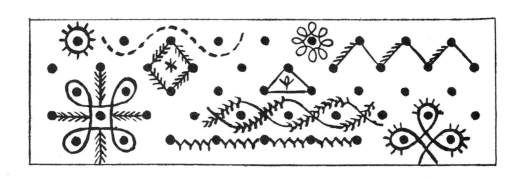

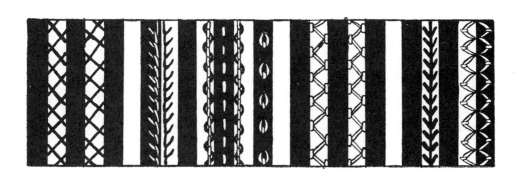

Some ways of elaborating patterned fabrics

so that they all appear as if they belonged to the animal and the spacing is pleasing to the eye.

From there you could try cutting holes inside the felt shapes, smaller circles or squares or leaf shapes. Remember to hem round both inside and outside when stitching them on. A further progression would be to make elaborate felt shapes which could be applied to a greater part of the body or the neck—perhaps fancy bands round the neck —and even down the leg. These too could have additional shapes cut inside them so that the background felt shows through. To make a really wonderful toy with elaborate decorations one could go even further and work appropriate embroidery stitches on to and round the appliqué.

Further on I have included some stitches which I think may be suitable for use on toys. Simple spots built up and enlarged with embroidery would be quite charming— there is no end to the richness of pattern and colour one can achieve with the use of several stitches.

Another method which is truly delightful is to use several thicknesses of cotton— these may be all in one colour or several colours. The contrast in texture is the chief joy of this method—perhaps fine sewing cotton next to thick soft cotton and a feathery stitch allied with a firm rigid stitch. When deciding what stitches to use I have found it a good plan to think about the skin or covering of the animal. This often makes your decision easier as several stitches can themselves suggest the texture of the creature. For instance feather or fly stitch look well if you wish to suggest the plumage of a bird, and detached chain can give a speckled effect. These of course are only isolated instances, but the toymaker herself will be able to devise many exciting combinations of stitches. Using them in different ways you can make scales, stripes, spots, feathers or what you will.

A wonderful piece of decoration is possible with the use of coloured beads and sequins. These may be purchased in a great variety of colour, size and shape. Toys enriched with such jewels are primarily to look at and are not suitable as playthings. Children tend to tear off the beads and eat the sequins. That is a great trouble with eyes made from beads or imitation eyes on wires—children are inclined to chew them out, so I would advise an embroidered eye for your creature.

Just as with embroidery, so beads and sequins can suggest the texture of a creature. For instance, overlapping sequins might look like scales, or a single one could suggest a glittering eye.

It is a good plan to keep your beads and sequins as part of the design on the animal whether they are allied with embroidery or not, instead of just spattering them about at random. If they are used carefully with an embroidered stitch they can do much to enhance it instead of detracting from it and making a confused pattern. A concrete suggestion might be to stitch long beads between the arms of a continuous fly stitch, or to stitch tiny round beads on the end of buttonhole points.

EXTRA DETAILS

One last word about detail. As your toys become more elaborate you will certainly wish to include more interesting detail such as trappings on horses, a howdah on an elephant, baskets on a donkey, etc. These details are as important as the toy itself, and they must be suitable in size and scale. Detail which is too big immediately looks ugly and clumsy and the toy is better without it. Always experiment with different sizes before you make your final choice. Some suggestions for harnesses might be twisted or knotted cords, stitched strips of fabric, pieces of felt cut with the pinking shears or a crochet chain of embroidery cotton, but always scaled to fit the toy.

MOUNTING ON PAPER

Before going on to stitches useful for assembling toys I should mention the best way to use fabrics that tend to fray. I think felt, very firm velour, leather and american cloth are the only materials which can be sewn without a turning at all. If there is any likelihood of frayed edges, mount each separate part of the pattern on to a piece of cartridge paper. This keeps the pieces in shape. It means a little extra work but the result is worth it.

You must cut out each piece of the pattern in drawing paper to the exact size, then each piece of fabric $\frac{1}{4}''$ bigger on all edges. Tack the fabric to the paper, turning the extra $\frac{1}{4}''$ over on to the wrong side. On all inside curves and sharp points you will have to clip the fabric so that it lies flat on the paper with no bulges or wrinkles. When tacking use a very fine needle and thread so that when the tacking stitches are finally removed no holes show in the fabric. One can embroider right through the paper if necessary as it need not be removed, unless of course the toy is to be washed. Then gently tear away the paper except along the edges where the turning has been tacked down. I find that the cartridge paper often gives a toy an extra bit of body and helps it to keep its shape.

Very large toys do not need this paper base as you can allow bigger turnings and are often able to machine or backstitch them on the wrong side. With smaller toys this is not practicable, so they must be stitched on the right side. It must follow then that this stitching must be neat, firm and accurate. Make certain that the parts of the toy fit together by pinning it here and there. Too many pins are a nuisance, so sometimes I tie a thread at the beginning, at the end, and in two or three places in between the two sections which are to be stitched together. Pay particular attention to curved edges, especially inside curves where you have had to snip the fabric. For these places the sewing should be close so that there will be no pulling away when you start to stuff the toy.

ASSEMBLING STITCHES

The most usual methods of assembling are shown on page 9. First we have a simple *seaming stitch*. This makes a very neat, firm edge when a fine thread is used. Keep the stitching small and even. It may be used on either wrong or right side. Sometimes a contrasting thread looks quite well if the sewing is regular. If you are assembling a silk or taffeta toy with this stitch, make sure your sewing thread is not too hard or coarse or it will tear the fabric. One or two strands of stranded cotton are usually strong enough.

Then there is *running stitch*. This is best used on felt or on material that does not fray. You will probably find it difficult to run the needle along the two thicknesses of felt, so *stab* it through from back to front of the seam, keeping it perfectly straight and taking care to see that the stitches appear straight and even on both sides. This kind of assembling stitch may be further enhanced by whipping with a second colour, or threading it with a contrast or even threading along one way with one colour and back again with a third. A further addition to an edge which has been stab-stitched together could be a buttonhole stitch worked along the raw edge.

Buttonhole itself is quite suitable for holding a seam, and even varieties of this are possible—*vandyke buttonhole* or *knotted buttonhole* (see pp. 16, 17) could be used. It is advisable to use a fairly close stitch, though, so that no stuffing will peep through or the seam look clumsy. Sometimes a buttonhole stitch may be worked along each edge of the separate parts of the toy and then the two edges laced together with the same or a contrasting colour. If you choose this method your buttonhole stitching should be very even or the lacing will be difficult.

Saddle stitch makes a firm edge and again it is best used with felt. First work a stab stitch along the seam, and then work back along the same seam with the same stitch, filling in the spaces you left on the first journey. This too looks well worked in two colours. Take care to put your needle into the same holes each time so that the stitch appears alike on both sides.

You may prefer to *oversew* your seams on the outside. This is similar to the fine seaming I first mentioned. The stitch is a little larger but the method of working is the same. Put the needle through the seam perfectly straight at even intervals, and you will have a sloping stitch showing. Worked in a contrasting colour it forms a good edge.

Crossed oversewing is a variation of the single oversewing. Just work your first line of stitching as I have described and make a return journey using the same holes, placing your needle straight through them, and the sloping stitch will cross over the first row. This looks attractive worked in two colours, but do be accurate with the spacing of the stitch.

Fishbone is a good method for fastening two seams together. It is the least bulky and makes for a very flat seam. It is suitable too for stitching small parts of patchwork toys together. Hold both pieces of fabric together flat and edge to edge. Then bring the needle through from the back a little way below the edge of the lower piece of material. Next make a vertical stitch, putting the needle under the upper piece and bringing it out a little way above. Then repeat the same thing but this time pointing the needle downwards and placing it under the lower piece of fabric and bringing it out level with the first stitch. This is not nearly so complicated as it sounds. A better seam is made if the stitches are fairly close together, when there will be no holes through which stuffing could escape.

Finally I would like to mention a very good method of finishing seams. Sometimes a plain stitched join is not enough or perhaps a little untidiness has crept in—particularly if the fabric has been difficult to handle. In cases like this I would advise *couching* a second thread round all the seams. You may use a stranded cotton, a soft cotton or even a very fine cord, and you could couch it in a variety of ways either with a finer thread or one of the same thickness. You will find some of these ways on page 18. This does tend to emphasize the shape of the toy and very often gives it a compact and completely finished look.

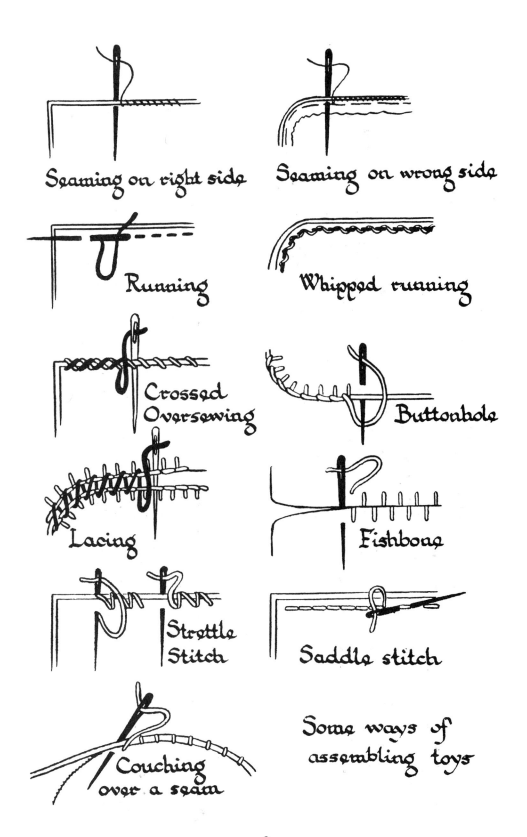

Seaming on right side

Seaming on wrong side

Running

Whipped running

Crossed
Oversewing

Buttonhole

Lacing

Fishbone

Strettle
Stitch

Saddle stitch

Couching
over a seam

Some ways of
assembling toys

A word about starting and fastening off. As a rule I find a safe method is to work a few running stitches first on the wrong side in the opposite direction to the line of work. Sometimes one can start with a knot on the wrong side, but it must be quite secure and I would suggest an extra stitch into the material before starting on the seam. To fasten off, either work an extra stitch over the last one and then run the thread along the inside, or work back over several stitches, taking care to cover them exactly so that no fastening off can be seen.

EMBROIDERY STITCHES

I am including some embroidery stitches which are suitable for toys. No doubt you will know many more, but perhaps these will jog your memory or serve as an inspiration for experiment. I have not suggested ways of combining them, as different patterns of stitching will occur to you when you once start to think about your toy. Those who know very few stitches I hope will be encouraged to delve deeper into the craft of embroidery.

First we have *running stitch* and some variations of it (page 11). When it is worked evenly and accurately it can be very beautiful, so do not despise it because of its simplicity. You can whip it with another colour and make an attractive cord-like line of stitching. If you work *whipped running* do be careful not to have the running stitches too large, or the whipping will look loose and clumsy.

Then your running stitch may be *threaded*—that is taking a second thread, of a different colour if you wish, and threading it up under one stitch and down under the next and so on. Be careful with the tension here—not too slack or the stitch will not stay in place. It should have a gentle curve. This threaded running may be varied too. You could thread one colour along one way and a second one along the other, so having a series of loops which are tied down with the running. Then again try double rows of running, and whipping or threading those. These give a much thicker line of stitching. Do see however that the two rows of running have their stitches exactly under each other.

Another kind of running stitch is *Holbein stitch*. This consists of a row of running worked in the usual way with the spaces and stitches of even length and then a second row worked back over the first, filling in the spaces with the second stitches. Variations of Holbein stitch are possible too. One can make turret shapes or have sloping offshoot stitches ; these should be worked in with the first row of running and care must be taken to see that the stitches and pattern are the same on the wrong side as on the right.

The next group of stitches is that based on the *backstitch* (page 12). This is useful itself, but you may add to it, making it thicker and richer. The simplest addition is that of threading a second colour through the basic stitch as in threaded running. This looks very well worked in two different thicknesses of thread—a fine one for the back-stitch and a much thicker one for the threading. *Pekinese* is another form of threading but needs more care with the tension. Then a thicker braid-like stitch is *interlaced backstitch*. This is a threading worked over two rows of backstitch. The stitches on these rows must be exactly underneath each other or the interlacing will not work out evenly.

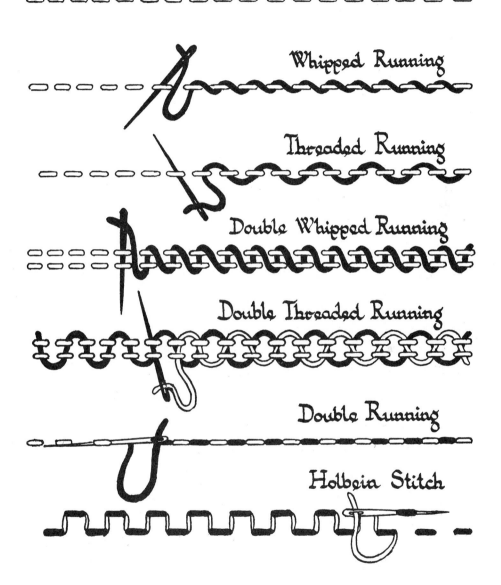

Running

Whipped Running

Threaded Running

Double Whipped Running

Double Threaded Running

Double Running

Holbein Stitch

Backstitch

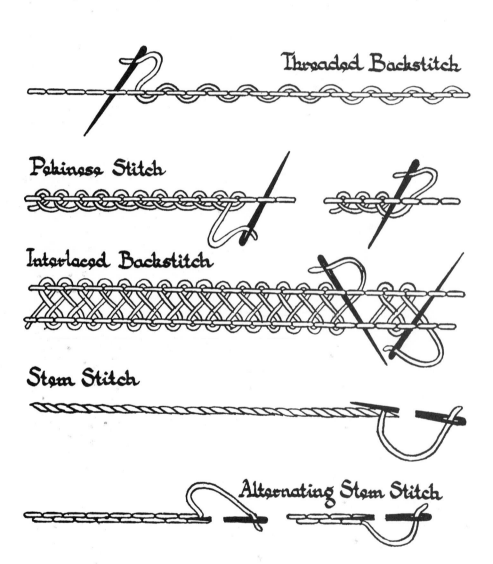

Threaded Backstitch

Pekinese Stitch

Interlaced Backstitch

Stem Stitch

Alternating Stem Stitch

Stem stitch is similar to backstitch, in fact if it is worked correctly a backstitch should be formed on the wrong side. These fine narrow stitches are particularly suitable on small toys as they can be used for tiny designs without fear of clumsiness. *Alternating stem* is a variation of the original stem and makes a slightly thicker line. The stitches must be of uniform length or the work loses its charm. Work exactly as a stem stitch but change the thread to alternate sides of the needle with each stitch.

Chain stitch in its many varieties (pages 14 and 15) is always a useful and decorative stitch. It gives such a beautiful, firm, rigid line and may be worked into small patterns. Keep the stitch neat and even and not too big.

Whipped chain makes a raised cord-like line and here again you can use more than one colour.

Detached chain is good for filling spaces, suggesting spots or speckles or for making a broken line. Sometimes detached chain threaded with one or two colours looks well. This gives a wider line of decoration. One could even add further stitching in the spaces to give a richer effect.

Then we have *magic chain* worked with two colours threaded into the needle at the same time. Varying sequences of colour are possible, depending on which thread is placed under the needle when making the stitch.

Zig-zag chain gives a pretty, broken line, but do remember to catch down the edge of the previous stitch with the needle when making the second and subsequent stitches, or you will find them slipping out of place.

Twisted chain makes a slightly looser line and has a rope-like appearance.

Cable chain is a dainty stitch with small loops along it. Keep it fairly small or it will become ugly.

Then we come to the more complex chain stitches. *Open chain* has a broader line and looks like a ladder. This could be worked over several thicker background threads as a sort of couching.

Double chain is a lovely stitch with the quality of braid. It gives a wider line and it may be used for filling small spaces. If allowed to become too wide it becomes ugly. Remember to fasten down both of the last stitches of the line to prevent them from slipping back.

Zig-zag cable chain is a variation of the straight stitch and makes a very attractive broken line. You could work it in single lines or double ones, making a series of chevrons or diamonds, depending on the arrangement of the zig-zag. Further stitching may be added to the spaces of the diamonds.

A truly delightful stitch is *crested chain* and is quite easy to work as long as you remember that it has three stages. Keep the coral knot at the left side and see that it is small, taking up only a small fraction of fabric. Then slip the needle under the sloping thread and finally work a biggish chain stitch on the line of work. Crested chain is very good worked on the outside curve of a circle, but it does need careful spacing.

The last of the chain stitches which are illustrated is *rosette chain*—another charming stitch. It does however tend to slip a little if disturbed. Once again the tension is most important. The best results come from stitches which are worked fairly close together.

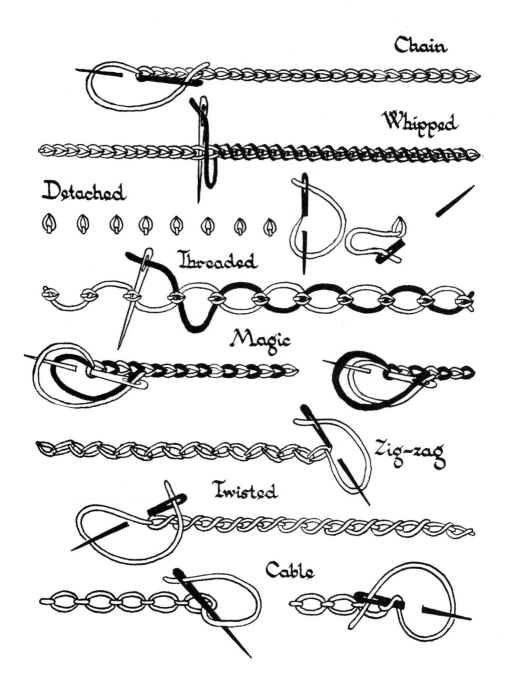

Chain

Whipped

Detached

Threaded

Magic

Zig-zag

Twisted

Cable

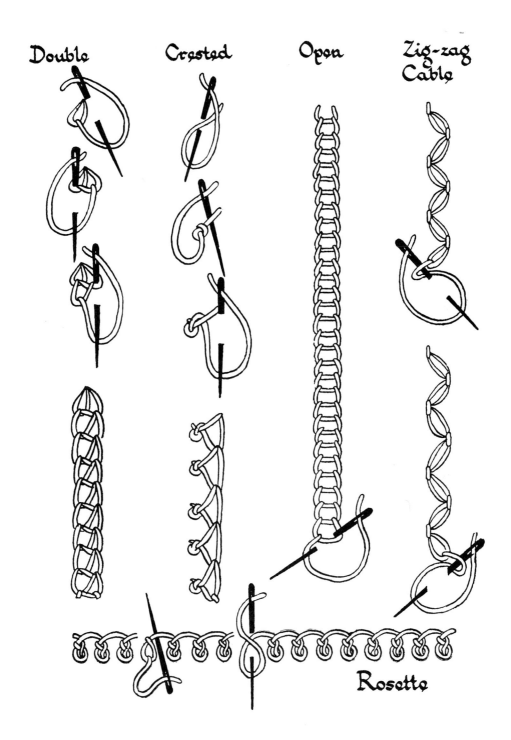

Double   Crested   Open   Zig-zag Cable

Rosette

Buttonhole stitch (page 17) is very useful and extremely simple to work. Even the straight type can be varied in several ways. It may be worked open or close, with long and short stems or in groups of close long stems alternating with groups of short stems and so on. Sometimes the bar along the bottom is whipped with another colour.

Vandyke buttonhole is charming and is good allied with other stitches. It gives a lovely delicate line of stitching. *Crossed buttonhole* is very similar but not quite so easy to work evenly. Try to make both bars of the cross the same length.

The *knotted buttonhole* needs care when working so that the knot and bar lie firmly on the fabric. When the needle is making the vertical stitch draw up the thread to tighten the knot before pulling the needle through.

I mentioned *couching* earlier as a form of decoration, but you need not stop at couching a single thread. Several thicknesses couched down look well and a number of stitches may be used to tie them, such as varieties of buttonhole, open chain, cross stitch or others which you may prefer (see page 18).

Cross stitch itself is useful worked separately or continuously. It is particularly effective on checked fabric where one can build up patterns by blocking out chosen squares with cross stitches. Try to make the threads all lie the same way.

Coral knot is especially good for small intricate lines or on small pieces of fabric which are difficult to hold. *Zig-zag coral* is a pleasing variation of the straight kind. See that the thread is twisted correctly when working the stitch at the right-hand side.

French knots are invaluable in embroidery. Worked separately or in thick clusters, or in conjunction with other stitches, they always look attractive. Do keep them firm, neat and round and not long and slack, when they will look untidy.

The last knot is *bullion knot*. It is a little more difficult to manage but if worked carefully looks extremely well. Several stitches worked close together give a thick raised effect.

Herringbone (page 19) is a broad stitch and although simple in method needs accurate spacing. It may be worked open or closed and is sometimes a basis for threading and interlacing. Two rows, a second colour worked over and in the spaces of the first row, make a thick interesting stitch. When working herringbone round a circle take care with the spacing. You will need to take a bigger stitch on the outside curve and a smaller one on the inside to ensure the stitch spreading evenly round the circle.

We have another zig-zag stitch in *chevron*. It is rather a stiff stitch and care must be taken with the arrangement of it if you are fitting it into a space. Rows worked the same way give a pleasant zig-zag or a neat diamond shape depending on how you place the short stitches at the top and bottom. Other stitches worked inside the diamonds will enrich the chevron.

Now we come to *fly stitch* (page 21) which is easy to work and attractive in appearance. *Continuous fly* may be worked open or close, depending on whether you want a delicate or solid effect. You can whip the centre stitch with a second colour and make a thick rope-like line down the middle.

Another variation is *chain and fly* when there is a chain instead of the straight stitch down the middle. This gives a much heavier line than the usual fly stitch. It is often whipped in the same way.

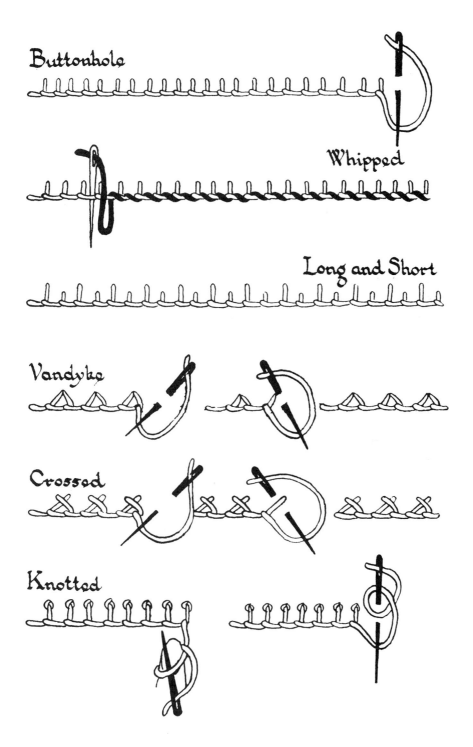

Buttonhole

Whipped

Long and Short

Vandyke

Crossed

Knotted

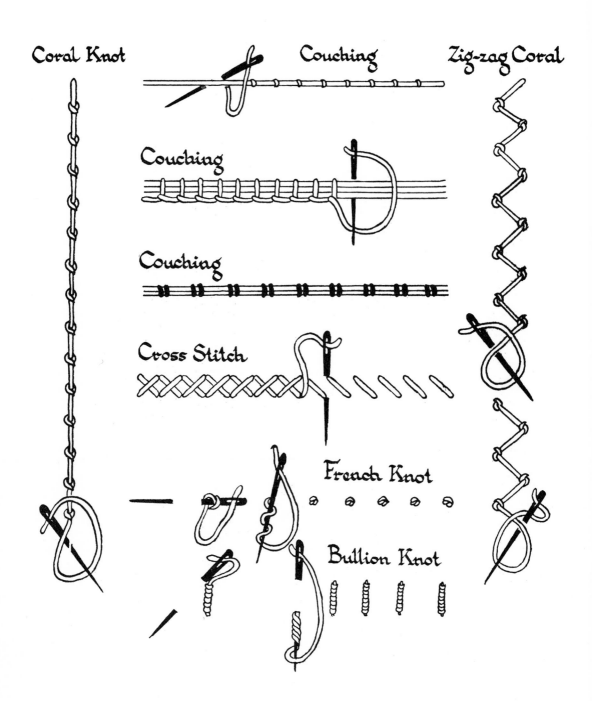

Coral Knot

Couching

Zig-zag Coral

Couching

Couching

Cross Stitch

French Knot

Bullion Knot

18

Herringbone

Threaded

Double

Closed

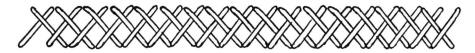

Chevron

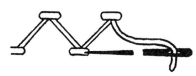

Single fly worked separately or in a continuous line gives a pretty edge and is also charming when used as a filling. *Single fly and chain* is similar in type. It makes a weightier filling than French knots or detached chain.

The last set of stitches I have included are the *feather stitches* (page 22). With the exception of *single feather*, which has only one arm, they are all broad stitches. Each one needs particular care with spacing. Often a row of feather stitch is spoiled because the spaces are too big. It is essentially a rhythmical stitch and until you master this rhythm the arms will never be even.

Double feather is a progression from the original stitch and makes a pleasing zig-zag line. The *long-armed feather* has, as its name suggests, a long stroke at each side with the needle emerging almost on the centre line making a little straight stitch along the middle.

Cretan is a kind of feather stitch, but the needle is inserted into the fabric almost horizontally. The stitches are usually worked fairly close together and the result is a plaited effect down the centre. This stitch is often used as a filling.

Chained feather stitch is a combination of two stitches and is best worked between two lines. It makes a wide border which is bold and attractive. One must watch the position of the needle carefully.

Finally we have *Spanish knotted feather stitch*. This is more complicated and if you have not tried it before work it on a scrap of material first so that you can master the tension and rhythm. The stitch is made by sloping the needle downwards and slightly to the left of the line of work, and the thread is looped round as in a coral knot. For the next point make a similar stitch sloping the needle to the right, but first of all inserting it just above the place where the threads cross in the stitch you have just made. If you keep it fairly compact you will have a beautiful, thick and rich braid-like stitch.

You no doubt will have many more stitches than these at your command, but I think those I have mentioned form a good basis for the decoration of toys. The ideal thing is to choose the appropriate stitch for your design and to be able to combine several lines of stitching to make an attractive whole. Many of these line stitches could be used as fillings for solid shapes on your patterns, so do experiment with different ones. You will be surprised at the lovely effects one can create by using a little thought and ingenuity.

Just a word of warning about starting and finishing. To start, run in a few stitches opposite to the line of work and to finish run your needle and thread through stitches on the wrong side. Do not carry the thread along the back from one line to another unless the distance is very short. If you have loops of thread along the back you will most certainly have trouble with the stuffing. Knobs of stuffing become fastened under these threads and the stuffing stick catches on them as well. The embroidery is pulled and puckered and sometimes the stuffing is difficult to dislodge.

STUFFING

The stuffing as a general rule is best put in in small quantities even if the toy is quite large. In this way you can pack it down evenly and avoid a lumpy appearance. Large wads of stuffing knot together, and instead of having a smooth surface to your toy you have a series of bumps. With the small toys put the tiniest bit of stuffing on the end of

Fly Stitch   Whipped Fly Stitch   Chain and Fly

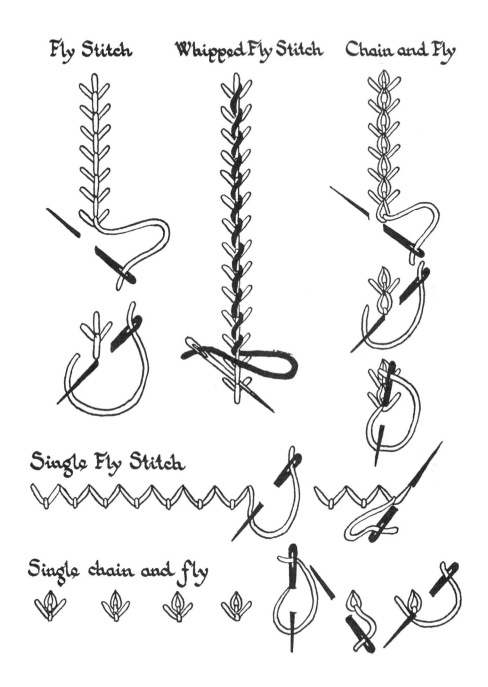

Single Fly Stitch

Single chain and fly

21

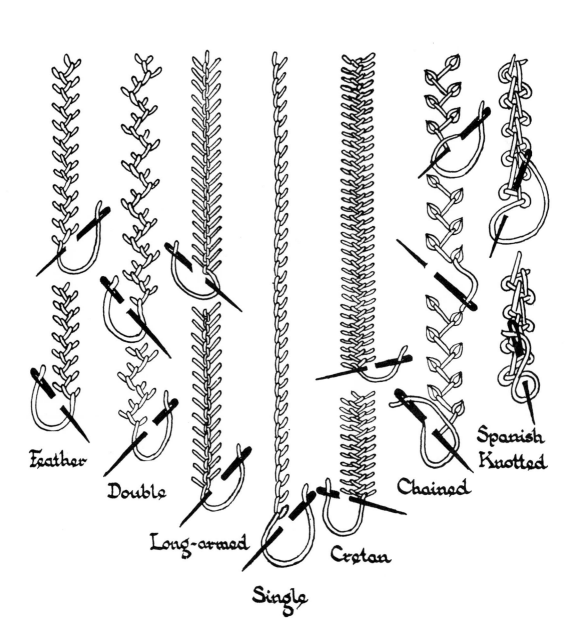

Feather

Double

Long-armed

Single

Cretan

Chained

Spanish
Knotted

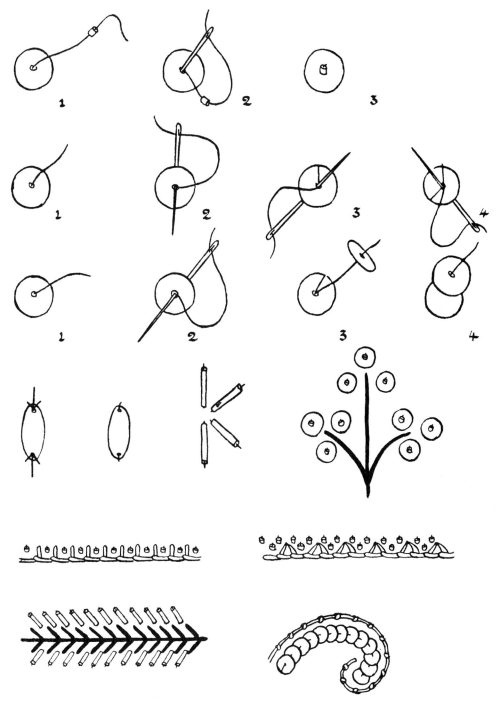

Some methods of sewing on beads and sequins

23

your knitting needle or skewer and push it gently but firmly into position, taking care to fill all corners. These are best stuffed first.

I find kapok the best stuffing as it is light and packs down very well, but cotton wadding—if it is teased out a little and the skin taken off—is quite good. A mixture of cotton waste called " Fluffydown " packs in well but makes a slightly heavier toy. I have sometimes used scraps of material cut into small pieces, or pieces of foam rubber. This latter makes quite a heavy toy and is not so easy to pack down.

OTHER POINTS IN MAKING

I would like to mention the sewing on of beads and sequins. Use a very fine needle and thread and be accurate in placing them. Sometimes it is more convenient to sew these on after the toy has been stuffed, as the assembling thread does tend to become caught round them. Most of these jewels have holes already pierced but if not it is a simple matter to poke a fine needle through them. Page 23 shows how to sew on sequins with or without beads, individually or in continuous lines. Once again watch the size of the beads and sequins in relation to the size of the toy. If they are too large the toy will look tawdry, clumsy and overdecorated.

There are one or two methods for transferring your design on to the toy. You may draw the pattern on quite freely with a piece of French chalk or sharp pencil or crayon, or you could cut out solid shapes from paper and draw round these on the fabric. If the fabric is woolly you could first draw out your design on tracing paper and tack it through on to the fabric, or you could trace it through with a coloured transferring paper. Sometimes I dot the design with a sharp pencil or stylo instead of drawing along the lines. On the whole the dotted pattern is easier to put on as you can exert more pressure.

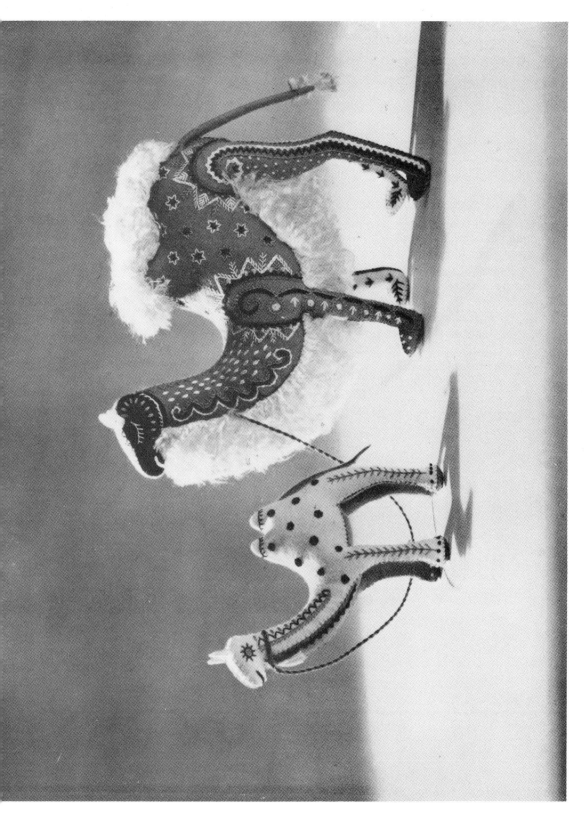

PLATE 1

Section Two

BALLS

THE SIMPLEST FORM OF TOY to make is the ball. Even young children can assemble these fairly rapidly and successfully. I think it is important that children are successful with their first attempt, so let it be something which is simple. Then they will have sufficient confidence and encouragement to try more difficult toys. Better still, with a large measure of success they will experiment with their own patterns, designs and fabrics. All the balls are made from felt. The more sections there are in the ball the rounder will be the result.

FOUR-SECTIONED BALL

The four-sectioned ball (page 26) does not give a perfect round, but there are only a few pieces to handle. It is so quickly assembled that your children do not become tired and bored before they reach the end.

Cut two sections in white felt and two in red. Then decorate each white section with small black circles of felt. To make these all even draw round a sixpence with a piece of French chalk or white crayon. Cut them out smoothly without leaving any corners on the edges. Then arrange them symmetrically in the two sections—about ten on each—and hem them on with a matching thread.

For the red sections cut out a star from white felt. Try it in paper first and draw round it. Hem it on to the centre of the section. Sew the sections together with a running stitch in black *coton-à-broder*. Make sure that the ends are pinned together before assembling and you will have a neat join where all four sections come together.

SIX-SECTIONED BALLS

The six-sectioned ball (page 27, left) is made from alternate sections of black and yellow and decorated with felt flower shapes. Cut these in paper first and draw round them on the felt. Turquoise shapes for the yellow pieces and cerise for the black. Arrange them evenly and hem on with a fine matching thread. A little further decoration may be added with some star Sylko. The large turquoise flowers have a whirl of white running stitch in the centre and spokes of black fly stitch in the spaces between the petals. The small turquoise shapes have a star of white straight stitches all going into the same central hole in the middle and black detached chain in the petal spaces.

The embroidery is a little different in the cerise flowers. On the large one we have eight detached chain in the centre and a second eight further towards the edge, all in white with lemon fly stitch spokes as in its turquoise counterpart. The small cerise one has a circle of white buttonhole in the centre and lemon detached chain in the spaces between the petals. All sections are stitched together with fishbone in turquoise. Be

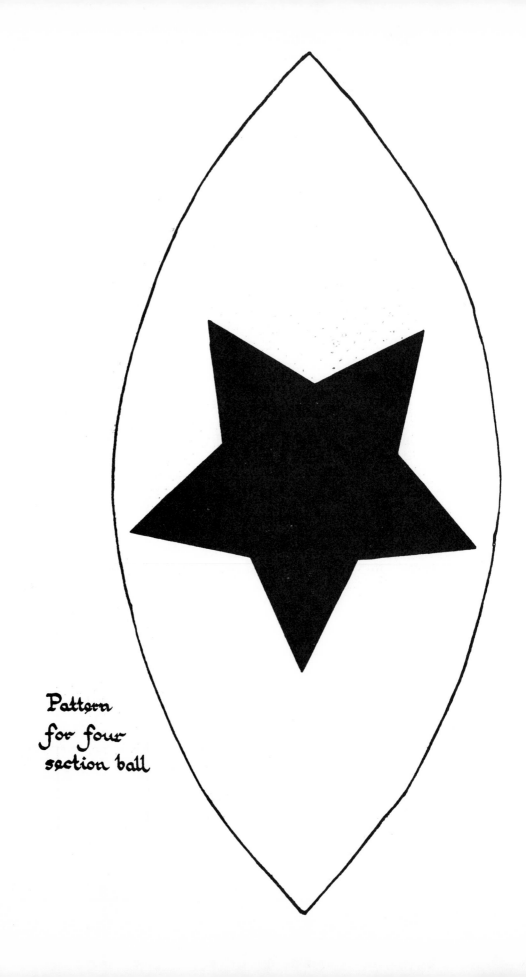

Pattern
for four
section ball

Pattern
for
six section
ball

27

careful that all the ends fit together.   If you have trouble in making a neat join where all the sections meet, make two more small felt flower shapes and stitch them over the two ends, adding a little embroidery to correspond with the rest.

The second six-sectioned ball (page 27, right) is more complex.   Each segment is made with three pieces.   You will see from the pattern that at each end there is a piece cut down in the form of a V.   All the end sections are in black while the centre pieces of the segment are in orange and turquoise alternately.   Cut all the pieces accurately and you will have no trouble fitting them together.   The black pieces are stitched in place with white fishbone.

Now the sections are ready for decoration.   There is a central stalk running right down each section.   On the black and orange piece this stem is worked in white fly stitch on the black felt, changing to white chain on the orange.   The leaf shapes are applied black felt.   Alternate ones are worked with a white buttonhole edge with a turquoise running and detached chain on the leaf itself.   The others have a turquoise chain surrounding them with a white fly down the middle.   On the black ends we have a turquoise felt circle with orange single fly round the edge and four black detached chain in the centre.

There are white applied leaves on the turquoise sections.   These are worked with orange detached chain along the centres with black vandyke buttonhole round the edge.   The alternate ones have an orange feather stitch on the underside with a black chain stitch leaf shape worked in the middle.   On the black ends we have an orange applied circle surrounded with turquoise single fly and four white detached chain in the middle.

Once all the sections are finished assemble them with black fishbone, having the white leaves pointing upwards and the black ones downwards.   Over the joins at top and bottom sew an orange circle and embroider it with a circle of white single fly and four turquoise detached chain.   This should complete a pleasing black star shape, formed by the black sections with their coloured circles at the top and bottom of the ball.

EIGHT-SECTIONED BALLS

The eight-segmented ball (page 29) has narrower pieces which are a little more difficult to handle.   The first one comprises alternate sections of blue and white with embroidered leaves and circles.   Cut out a leaf shape in stiff paper and draw round it on the felt, two on each section.   For the circle draw round a small thimble or similar object.

Four strands of stranded cotton are used for the stitching.   All the leaves are worked with red chain on the outside and red buttonhole on the inner leaf shape with black single fly between them.   A close white fly stitch fills the centre of them on the blue sections and a blue fly stitch on the white sections.   The circles are worked in white on the blue and the opposite way on the white.   These are spiders' webs.   Make eight straight stitches in the form of a star into a central hole and then work backstitches round these strands—do not take up any fabric—starting from the centre and working towards the outside until all the spokes are covered.   Stitch the sections together with black fishbone.

The last eight-sectioned ball (page 29) has a greater number of colours.   Each segment is divided by a sloping line across the middle.   Then four sections have black and pink joined together and four have grey and white—all joined by fishbone.

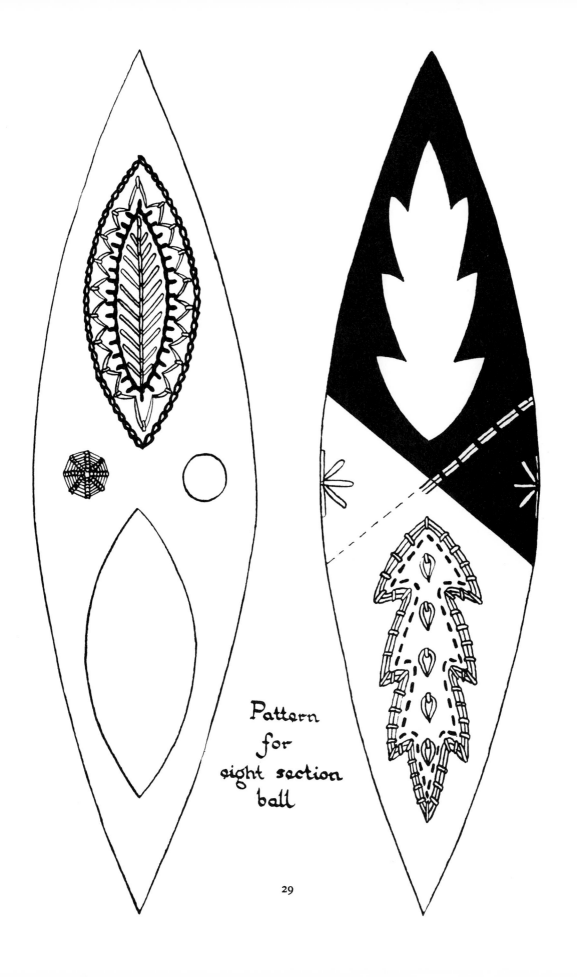

Pattern
for
eight section
ball

Cut a leaf shape with a serrated edge and draw round it on each colour. They are all worked in the same way—a double thick cotton thread couched round the outside of the shape—pink on white felt, black on grey felt, white on pink felt and grey on black felt. Detached chain stitches are worked in one thickness of thick cotton down the centres of the leaves in the same colours. Then a running stitch is made just inside the couched line, using three strands of stranded cotton. These are the colour combinations : black running inside the white leaf, pink inside the grey leaf, white inside the black leaf and grey inside the pink.

Stitch the sections together with fine white fishbone and arrange the segments so that no two pieces of the same colour come together. You will find that there is a zig-zag join now round the widest part of the ball. Cover this with a double couching of thick cotton in light turquoise and then couch a similar second zig-zag line crossing over the first and making diamond shapes. Work thick cotton stars of straight stitches in the middle of these diamonds in light and dark turquoise alternately.

Do not stop at these suggestions. Do try your own colour schemes and shapes to enrich the ball sections. Try cutting the sections in different ways to make patchwork balls—not too many pieces, though, or the ball will not stand much wear or tear. You will find your own designs really exciting and satisfying.

Section Three

ANIMALS

ANIMALS, LIKE MANY OTHER TOYS, probably originated as charms or idols and gradually became playthings. In some countries I believe it was the custom to present babies with different animal heads on sticks to act as charms to scare away various ills.

Home-made toy animals can be the most lovable and charming creatures, all with their own delightful peculiarities. You can make them more or less copies of the true animal or with a little ingenuity transform them into creatures of fun or fantasy. I have tried to grade the animal patterns, starting from the very simplest and leading to more difficult ones. The patterns which are included are only suggestions and the reader perhaps will work out her own ideas, and with the help of the methods I have described make her own patterns to suit her individual requirements.

Generally speaking it is a good thing to keep the shapes as simple as possible, avoiding intricate corners. Begin with a good side-view drawing, simplifying detail, much of which can be added with stitchery later on. Standing animals need fairly substantial legs, especially if they are for a toy to be made by children. Remember too that some of the thickness is taken up with the stuffing. The same thing applies to necks. When you have a good side shape you can then add gussets, etc., where necessary, e.g. where the animal has any particular thickness. I will explain about gussets as we come to them.

WIRING

I have talked about stuffing toys earlier in the book, but I did not mention the important point of wiring. Chunky or flat animals do not as a rule require any wire inside but most others do, particularly if the legs are slender. It is a simple matter to go up one leg, across the body and down the other plus a little extra (see page 32). Twist each end back on itself for about ¾″ and place the wire down the two front legs when the animal is partially stitched but not stuffed. Do the same for the back legs. If the creature has a long neck, twist a piece of wire for that and fasten it to the middle of the front legs piece. If there is any chance of the wire poking through the bottom of the feet, put a little stuffing in each foot first. Stuff very carefully round the wires, using small pieces of stuffing.

ANIMAL MANES

Before we go on to the actual animal patterns it might be useful to know some methods of making details such as tails, manes, etc. No doubt you will be able to adapt these I have included or they may stimulate you to try out others of your own.

Manes are important in animal structure. Do try to choose the kind that is most suitable for your creature. For instance a delicate lace mane would look out of place

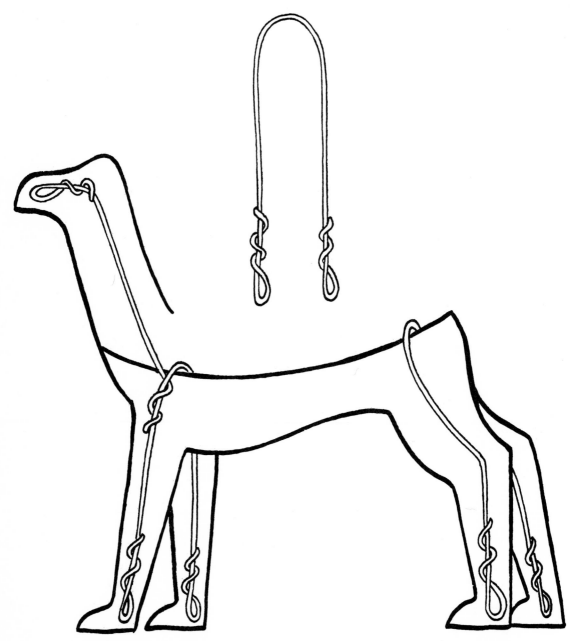

Method of twisting wire for a stuffed animal

on a heavy felt carthorse, but might be just right for a colt made from silk or fine cotton. These details often make or mar the creature and they deserve some careful thought. They must be related to the general design of the animal too and not appear to be stuck on as an afterthought.

Overleaf are shown some methods of making manes. First we have the simple cut-out shape from felt or leather—anything that does not fray. If you have a scalloped edge, draw round something circular and keep the scallops even. The pointed mane needs careful cutting too. The size of the points or scallops will be determined by the size of the animal. Two or even three rows may be used.

A similar mane can be made from fabric which frays by first mounting it on a paper shape cut to size. Fold over and tack down the edges, clipping right into the corners. Two of these stitched together wrong sides facing make an attractive mane. Embroidery added to the scallops or points makes a further pleasing decoration.

A fringed mane is possible with anything which does not fray. Cut a strip to the length and width required and cut in strips to within a short distance of the top with very sharp scissors. A variation of this method may be cut in double fabric having a fold at the fringed edge. Several small rows of either the single or folded fringes overlapping each other make another type of mane. Stitch the lower one down first and you will find it does not obstruct the stitching of the next one.

Another attractive and delicate mane is knife- or box-pleated lace. Tack the pleats in before stitching to the animal and then release them. Rows of net or fine fabric, provided the edges have been neatened, also look very well in pleats. Gathers may be used if you prefer them.

A fine fringe is made by winding thread round card. For a first attempt try this method with thick soft cotton or wool. Cut a piece of card the length and width of the mane. Then wind your thread round it, the strands being close together and side by side. If you want a thicker mane, make several layers. Stem stitch along the top of the threads, taking the needle right through so that all are caught. Then cut along the opposite edge and take out the card. A very fluffy mane is made when you use a stranded cotton or a cord. All the threads can be untwisted and fluffed out.

Next we have tassels arranged at intervals or very close together. Make your tassel by winding a thread round your fingers or a piece of card. Slip a thread under one end and tie a knot. Cut the other ends. Push the knot under the threads of the tassel and bind a second thread round to form a neck.

Loops of wool stitched straight on to an animal's neck make a good mane too. Take straight stitches through the fabric, leaving a slack loop on top. To be effective these should be fairly close together. A strip of fur is sometimes useful too or a raffia mane made in the same way as the silk fringed one. Once the manes are sewn on they may be clipped to size and shape with very sharp scissors.

ANIMAL TAILS

There are several ways (see page 36) of making tails. Twist a simple plait of wool, silk or raffia with a knot at the end. If you use this method put several strands of thread in the tail so that it will not look thin and stringy. Then there is the bound tail. Take a

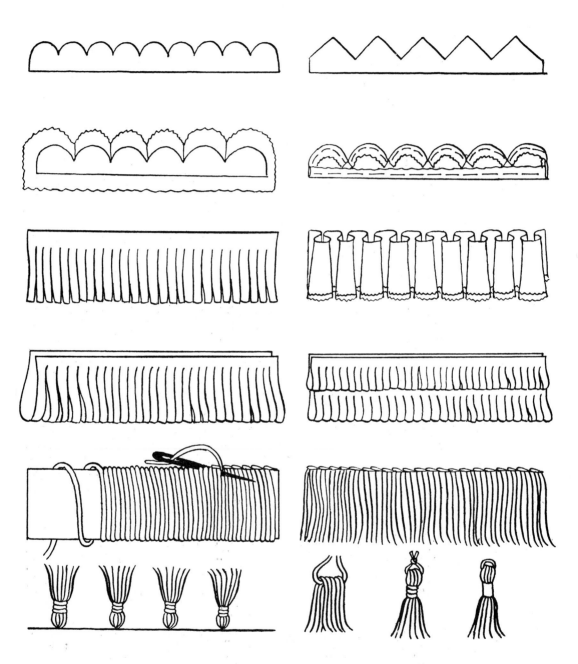

Some ways of making manes

few strands of cotton, wool or raffia, which looks well, and starting a little way from the end bind them tightly together, making all the binding threads lie side by side. Fasten off at the top by putting the binding thread into a needle and stabbing it backwards and forwards through the tail. This end would be put inside the animal, so the fastening off would not be seen.

A tapering felt tail is suitable for some animals. Cut a long, narrow, V-shaped piece of fabric with a rounded end at the top. Then fold it in half and stitch the two sides together as far as possible. The tail is then stitched to the body round the circular piece at the top.

Fringed felt or leather gives a good tail. Be generous with the felt and make a lovely sweeping tail. First cut a strip of material, fringe it, then roll it tightly, stitching through the roll to make it secure. This may be stitched to the outside of the body or the roll put inside with just the fringe showing. The other fringed tail is made with silk, cotton, wool or rayon thread as a normal tassel is made. Try different kinds of threads—nobbly ones or curly ones all give different styles of tail. A short tasselled tail looks just as well as the long one sometimes.

Wire serves as a convenient base for a tail because it can be bent or twisted into various positions. Millinery wire is good, or any one that is soft and pliable. To cover it with thread turn up one end to form a tiny loop. Lay the beginning of your thread along the double piece of wire and then start binding over the end of the thread and the two strands of wire. The loop may be enhanced with a tassel or small fringe.

Wire covered with fabric is another method. Fold a piece of material round the wire and seam along one edge. Knobs, discs, pom-poms, etc., may be added to the end if you wish. A wider tail is made by stitching a piece of wire between two layers of felt. Do this with running stitch on each side of the wire to hold it in position. Then cut your felt to its final shape. The sides could be fringed or cut into points or scallops.

A narrow double piece of felt, fringed and wound up, makes a short blob of a tail. A circle of fur or lambswool with a knob of cotton wool in the centre makes a rabbit's tail. Run a gathering thread round the outer edge and pull it up tightly.

Another stuffed tail is made by cutting two U-shaped pieces of fabric and stitching round them. No doubt other ways of making tails will occur to you as you create your animals.

ANIMAL EARS

There are a few suggestions for making ears on page 37. The embroidery on them is usually determined by the shape of the ears themselves. If they are made in fabric which frays, remember to tack it on to the paper shape first. In this case you will need two sides stitched together with the paper inside. Often the inner ear is attractive in a different colour and with a different decoration. The tall rabbits' and donkeys' ears frequently need tailor's canvas inside for extra body.

Watch carefully the position of the ear. It can quite alter the animal's character and sometimes even its species! Notice too whether the ear stands up, is folded or fairly flat, hangs down or lies back over the head. These details are all important. An ear with a cavity may be suggested by folding the fabric from each side up to the middle,

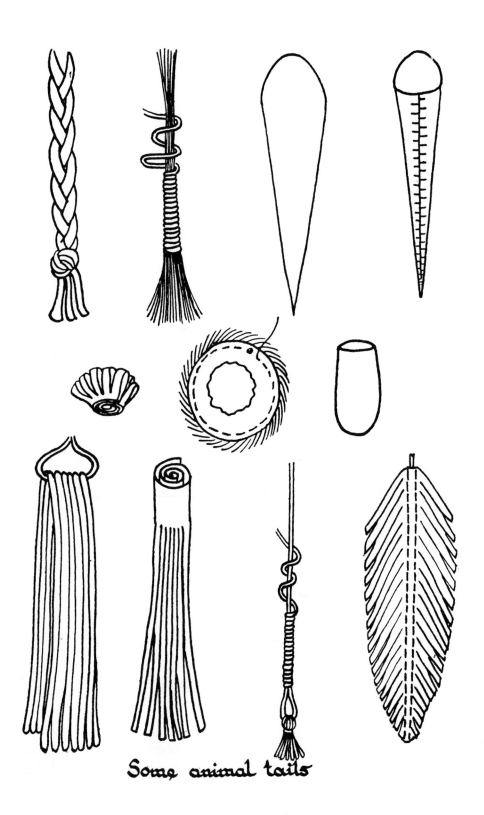

Some animal tails

Fold Fold

Animal ears

as in the diagram at the top of page 37, and secured with stitching, or by cutting a V in the base of the ear and stitching in a partially closed position on the creature. If the ear is large and floppy there is scope for decoration on the underside as well.

ANIMAL EYES

The eye is the key to the personality of the animal, so spend some time over deciding what kind of look it is to have. Is it to be kind and genial, ferocious, awe-inspiring, coy, disdainful, shy or sleepy? Very often the eye is pushed on at the last minute—indeed occasionally it is difficult to find at all, and the eye is important, so there should be no niggling or scrappy work. You can embroider it, apply pieces of fabric, make it from beads and sequins or have a combination of these methods. Odd buttons and beads come in useful. If the animal is a plaything an embroidered eye is best, as children are apt to pull off, suck and even swallow beads, buttons, glass eyes and their wires, etc.

The position of the eye should be accurate. If you are not certain look at a picture or ask your non-sewing friends to criticize. If it is not right they will notice immediately. If there is a pupil it should be correct in position too. It is very easy to make the creature look vacant or cross-eyed. Imagine it looking forward, upwards, downward or sideways, and place the pupil accordingly.

On page 39 there are some ways of working eyes. The first drawing shows an applied piece of felt for the pupil with French knots half-way round. This is enclosed in a circle of coral knot surrounded by single fly stitch and detached chain.

Then we have a more realistic-looking eye made from stem and small buttonhole. The pupil could be chain stitch worked solidly and surrounded by satin stitch. The upper lid is suggested with a second row of stem and a row of vandyke buttonhole.

Number 3 shows a closed eye with a fringe of lashes worked in long buttonhole. A row of chain higher up emphasizes the shape of the eye.

A decorative eye is made with a central sequin circled on three sides with long beads, with small ones spattered in between. A second less realistic eye consists of a central coil of coral within a circle of chain surrounded by a larger looped circle.

Number 6 shows an eye shape outlined with stem stitch in a double line to suggest the lid and finished with a line of sloping buttonhole for the upper lashes.

The next two show: first a V-shaped eye with an applied piece of felt for the pupil. This has stem stitch along the lower edge and a half-circle of chain above, then a V of chain and finally a V of crested chain. The other eye is a leaf shape of fishbone, running stitch and chain with buttonhole spreading around the lower edge.

A half-closed eye (9) is shown with the upper lid worked with rows of stem stitch finishing with vandyke buttonhole, and the lower lid worked with a fine straight buttonhole. The small piece of pupil that is showing could be in chain, satin or buttonhole stitch worked solidly. Then we have a sparkling eye made from a silver metal star with beads added to the spaces and scallops of coral knot looping round them.

Number 11 has the eye shape of stem along the upper and vandyke buttonhole along the lower edge. These are elaborated with branches of fly and long single fly stitches. The pupil consists of satin stitch surrounded by French knots or beads.

Another eye shape is shown in 12. It has a > shape worked in buttonhole followed

1   2   3

4   5   6

7   8

9   10   11

12   13   14

Some ways of working animal eyes

Decorative animal heads

Some more suggestions for decorating animals

up by the same in stem. The pupil is a half-circle of stem with a long single fly stitch filling it.

Then there is a sloping leaf-shaped eye of chain with a tail of fly stitch. The inner eye is of fine herringbone with a detached chain in the middle.

The last eye illustrated has a half-circle of small buttonhole with a tiny coil in the middle. There are further half-circles sweeping back above this in threaded backstitch, stem and vandyke buttonhole, and a smaller one below in stem. A stuffed eye could be sewn on to an animal which has prominent eyes, such as the frog or toad. Add the embroidery after it has been stitched in position.

HORNS

Horns are best cut to shape and stuffed. If they are long or liable to flop about, wire them. A twisted horn can be made from a very long stuffed tube which has been wired. After the stuffing twist the horn as you wish. The horns themselves look well with embroidery on them, braid twisted round, fringes or fur added. Some horns are best constructed from wire in the same way as tails, perhaps adding branches—a reindeer's horns for example. You could bind them or cover them with felt, or even decorate them with glittering sequins. Feathers or quills may be used too. One can even cut the stiff quills into different shapes.

Nostrils and mouths should be correct as to position. As a rule upturned mouths give a happy look while downturned ones look glum.

DECORATED HEADS

I have included some suggestions for decorating several kinds of animals' heads. First there is the elephant. Here you have scope for quite a lot of embroidery on the trunk—perhaps graduating the stitching as the trunk becomes narrower. Then there is the place where the tusk joins the body. If it has been difficult to sew on, your embroidery will neaten the edge. The elephant in the diagram on page 40 has an embroidered cap. You could work this directly on to the animal or on a separate piece and stitch it on later.

The camel has a head of quite a different shape. Here the stitching is carried round the division between the head and neck and a separate pattern worked down the neck. French knots and buttonhole make the mouth and a detached chain the nostril. Here the eye is open but a camel looks equally well with a disdainfully closed eye.

The head of the mountain goat is similar in shape and has been divided up in much the same way although the stitching is not the same. The ear slopes downwards from just outside the horns.

In the horse's head we have the embroidery carried right up the neck on to the face. A second set of stitching is worked on the front of the head. Do not get them too near the eye, or it will become lost in the confusion of stitching.

The goat with curved horns has them in two colours. The ear too has a contrast inside. The eye is simple but forceful. The zig-zag along the top of the face could easily be a piece of felt cut with the pinking shears. Then the appliqué could be continued down the neck in the form of small circles further enriched by surrounding embroidered patterns.

Simple dog pattern with two sides

The neck of the giraffe is similar and of course one can vary the shape of the markings, which may be applied or embroidered. Thinner stitching on the head is needed because of its more delicate shape. Use covered wire or painted wood for the horns.

The next creature has two colours for the body, each with its own design. The pattern on the head follows the line with a strong important eye. Once again the ears are in two colours, each with a different design.

The lion head is important largely because of the mane. In the diagram it has been made from rows of double-fringed fabric overlapping each other. A more realistic mane may be made from fringing cord or silk and unravelling it after stitching it on to the creature. See that the stitchery used for attaching the mane is neat and pleasing.

SIMPLE PATTERN FOR DOG

The first pattern I have included is for a dog which has only two sides (page 43). Keep the shape simple without too many projecting pieces. Cut cleanly and accurately. Young children should be able to tackle this animal without difficulty.

Work the embroidery before assembling the creature. It consists of straight stitches of thick cotton worked in a V pattern. Turret or triangle shapes would be suitable too. Stitch the two sides together with running stitch, and stuff. Fasten a strip of felt round the neck, also with running. Work a few straight stitches in black for the nose and mouth. Finally make a fringe of felt, roll it and stitch it on for the tail. The animal is best stuffed from the underbody.

The original was a reddish brown felt with white decoration and black was used to stitch it together. The collar was green and the tail black. This makes a flattish animal but is quite good for a beginning as there is very little to go wrong. It will not stand. You could however string several of these along a bar and make an attractive baby's toy.

DACHSHUND

The dachshund on page 45 is a very simple standing animal involving two side shapes and a long straight strip. Although these creatures may be made in other fabrics felt is the best. The side shape is more complex than that of the first creature, but still fairly easy to handle. Once again avoid sharp corners and intricate bends.

The decoration in this case is a thick thread couched down with a thinner one. With very young children a free pattern worked straight on to the fabric would look quite well, or one that has been pencilled or chalked on without any preliminary drawing.

Start and fasten off on the wrong side. Work the embroidery before making up the animal. When you have finished the embroidery, stitch one side to the strip with a seaming stitch, using either *coton-à-broder* or sewing cotton. Cut the strip to the correct length and stitch the two ends together. Then carefully mark with a dot various points along the open side of the strip. For instance the point opposite to where the nose comes and the front of each paw and the final join. These dots can then be matched to their appropriate places when you stitch on the other side. This is very important as this type of animal is liable to twist badly if the two sides are not exactly opposite each other. Some animals are improved with a little twist but not this one as it will not stand.

Leave open a space underneath and then stuff, starting with the head, then the legs

Tail

Ear

Dachshund pattern. Cut 2 sides and 1 strip

and lastly the body.   Stitch up the opening.   Finally add the ears and tail with a seaming
stitch along the top edge in each case.

This dog was made in light fawn felt, sewn together with a matching thread and
embroidered in white.   The eye and nose were black.

SIMPLE STANDING ANIMALS—REINDEER AND COW

The next group of animals have four legs and can stand too.   I am sure you have
all made those potato and matchstick pigs and horses in your youth.   Perhaps an oddly
shaped potato has inspired such a creature, with sticks for legs, twigs for horns and a
feather for a tail.   The animals I have included on page 47 are based on such originals,
each piece of the creature being made separately.   Naturally all the shapes are simple
and although the results are not entirely realistic they can embrace all the characteristics
of the real animal.

The first is a reindeer.   It has a tube for a body made from two circles of green felt
with a straight strip of striped fabric $5\frac{1}{2}'' \times 6\frac{1}{4}''$ joined up and then stitched to the circles.
The black and green striped material is embroidered with broken lines of white fly stitch
worked along the stripes.   The front circle has eight spokes of white fly stitch with black
detached chain in the spaces, while the back circle has a coil of black and white whipped
running.   The legs are four tubes of felt, green outside with white stitching and black
inside.   The head is two triangles, with rounded corners, of green felt, with a black eye
and mouth.   The head gusset is of striped fabric, with the narrowest part at the mouth.
All are stitched together with black sewing cotton.

See that the edges of the cotton fabric are turned in, and leave openings for stuffing
at one end of the body, the tops of the legs and the side of the head.   Stuff carefully.
Stitch on the legs at the top, matching them accurately.   Stitch on the head at the proper
angle—upright for the reindeer.   Then hem on the ears at each side, cut two quills and
stick them through the head for horns and make a fringed coil of green felt for the tail.
Fasten it in the middle of the back circle.   You will have a gay and amusing animal.

COW

Make a spotted cow in the same manner.   This time the legs will be shorter, the tail
longer and the head sewn on at a different angle.   The body is made from two oval
shapes for back and front—one marked with a circle of black fly stitch with a line of white
fly down the middle, the other with coils of white cable chain and black running.   A
piece of spotted fabric is suitable for the body.   Make it as for the tubular body of the
reindeer.   Alternate rows of spots are enriched with embroidery—black buttonhole round
a turquoise spot and then a row of cerise chain, and cerise chain round the spot with a
circle of black vandyke buttonhole.   The spots down the middle of the head gusset are
worked with cerise buttonhole with a line of black cable chain joining them up.   The
legs, tail, side head pieces and oval shapes are in cerise felt while the head gusset and body
are white cotton with turquoise spots.   When cutting the body piece see that the spots
are arranged evenly.

Dogs, cats, horses, deer may all be made on this principle.   One can make more
elaborate heads, legs and feet, put on greater detail and so make creatures of fantasy.

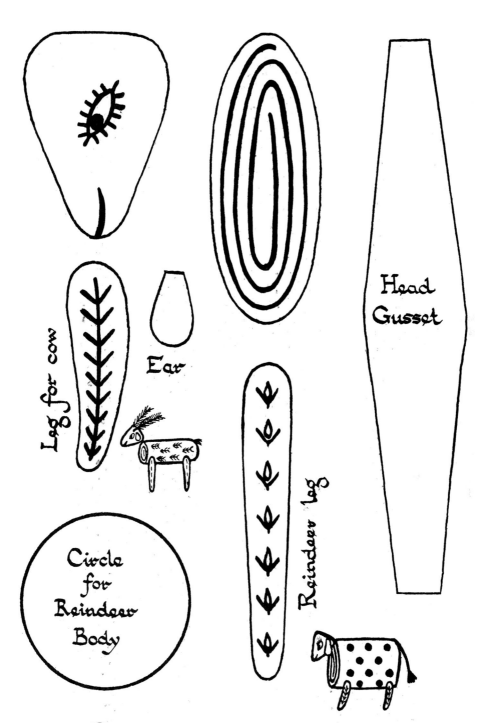

Head Gusset

Leg for cow

Ear

Circle for Reindeer Body

Reindeer leg

Pattern for cow and reindeer

47

ANIMAL WITH MOVABLE LEGS—HORSE

We now come to an animal with movable legs. The head, neck and body are all in one piece, involving a little more skill in shaping than in the previous pattern. The body has simple circles for decoration. Draw rings round any small round object—not necessarily the same size, spacing them suitably. Cut the shapes in blue felt and work the rings in white buttonhole with four black detached chain in the middle. *Coton-à-broder* or two strands of stranded cotton would be suitable. Then stitch the long strip round the body, remembering to mark various points round it as described in the making of the dachshund. The eyes, nose and mouth are worked in black. Each leg consists of two pieces of felt with three circles on the outer side of each. Embroider these in the opposite way from those on the body—black buttonhole with white detached chain. Sew round the legs, leaving a space open for stuffing. Stuff all five parts and finish them off. The assembling is done with a seaming stitch in a fine matching thread. Stitch on the small felt ears, folding them into a V shape at the bottom. The mane consists of three small white tassels of thick soft cotton. The tail is a larger tassel.

The legs are attached with a piece of very fine round elastic threaded through a stout needle. Push the needle through the body and then through the top of one leg, coming out in the centre of the embroidered motif. Then back the same way and through the second leg; back through this to where you started. Pull the two ends up tightly and tie in a firm knot. This will be hidden between the leg and the body.

DEER

The pattern of the deer (page 50) is the first example of an animal with a separate piece for the underbody, giving four legs. A great many toys are made with this method. It makes quite a realistic toy. Once again, though, keep the general outline fairly simple. You will see from the diagram the line which marks the top of the underbody. The legs are cut exactly to match those of the whole side view. When marking the line for the underbody it is best sloped slightly downwards in the middle. This does stop the legs from splaying too badly. I have not included a head gusset, but a small diamond-shaped piece stretching from the nose to just behind the ears could be added. Make the widest part on the top of the head and slope to a point for both the nose and neck ends. Almost any four-legged animal, providing it is not too solid or chunky a one, may be made with this method.

The original deer was made in two colours of felt, crimson for the outside and white for the underbody. Cut two sides from red felt and two undergusset sections from white. Seam along the top edge of the underbody on the wrong side. Sew small leaf shapes or spots cut from white felt on to the side pieces with a matching cotton. Fit the underbody to the two side pieces and seam round with red thread. Leave open the tail end and a little way along the back. These legs are rather slender, so you may wire them if you wish.

When stuffing use very small pieces at a time. Fill the head and neck first, then the front legs, back legs and finally the body. Sew up the opening. Fold the base of the ears to the middle and stitch, then sew on to the animal. Lastly work the eye and nose

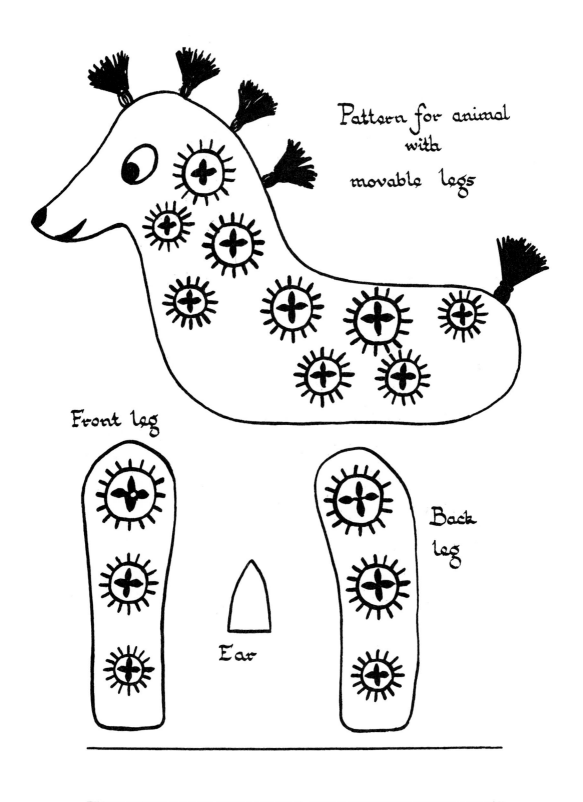

Pattern for animal
with
movable legs

Front leg

Back leg

Ear

Ear

Pattern for deer with undergusset

with black thread. Additional decoration could be added to the legs, the undergusset and the hooves if you wish.

The horse pattern (pages 52–4) is a further progression. This includes a gusset along the back which gives more thickness to the animal. I have also shown this same animal worked out in three different ways, from using an easily handled fabric like felt with a little decoration, to a design much more elaborate both in colour and shape worked on taffeta. In each case the initial pattern is the same—a very simple outline with little detail. You may adapt this how you will. For instance you may want a more realistic face—perhaps showing a little more of the curves of a horse's face—but if you are using the design with children, additional shaping makes the sewing more difficult. As well as a back gusset I have put in soles for the feet. These need not be used if you do not wish as the animal stands very well without them.

The first horse is made from blue, yellow and black felt. Cut out one side and one underbody piece in both yellow and blue. Cut the long back gusset in black. In the diagram this is in two sections but when you make your tracing draw it in one long piece. The embroidery is based on stars dotted over the body. These may be worked in any number of ways. For instance you could have five straight stitches to the centre with single fly stitch encircling them and detached chain in the spaces. For the lines down the leg any broad stitch would look well—feather stitch, fly, chained feather, etc. A similar stitch could be used for the line down the back gusset. For the coil on the soles of the feet, use a narrower stitch—whipped running, cable chain, threaded backstitch, etc. *Coton-à-broder* or three strands of stranded cotton in red, black and yellow on the blue, and red, black and blue on the yellow are used.

When the embroidery is complete, seam the two underbody gussets together on the wrong side. Then fit them to the two side shapes and stitch with strettle stitch in one of your colours. The long pointed end of the back gusset fits at the nose. Leave a space open for stuffing. You may wire this animal if you wish. Stuff the head and neck first, followed by front and back legs. Be careful to stuff firmly at the tops of the legs. It is easy to get a hollow at these points without any stuffing at all. If this happens the legs splay out and the animal will not stand.

The tail is two small pieces of felt stitched together and stuffed. The mane is two pieces of vandyked felt, one blue and one yellow, hemmed along the neck with matching thread. Hem on one yellow and one blue ear, folding them so that the bottom of the ear makes a V.

The second horse (page 53) is made from striped cotton fabric. In the main the stripes act as a background and are not used as a basis for the decoration. Dark grey and light grey stripes with a thin white line between were used for the original. On the sides and the underbody the stripes go down, and on the back gusset they go along. For this material you must cut out the shapes in paper first and cover each one with fabric —folding the turning over to the wrong side and tacking down. Clip the material at all the curves so that it lies flat and see that one side faces left and the other right.

Work the embroidery. White feather stitch for the line that goes down the neck

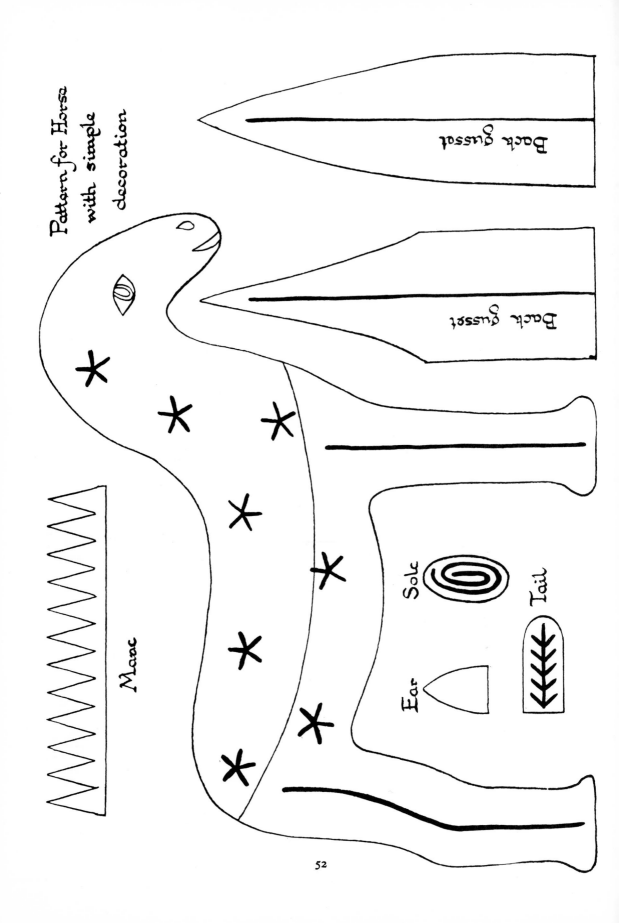

Pattern for Horse with simple decoration

Back gusset

Back gusset

Mane

Sole

Ear

Tail

52

Horse with more elaborate decoration and fringed mane and tail

53

Decorated horse
with trappings
and fringed silk
mane and tail

and finishes in a coil. Red chain stitch for the loops, black buttonhole for the circles, red fly stitch down the front of the nose gusset. The undergusset has black detached chain worked down alternate stripes. Seam the two underbody sections on the wrong side, then sew the whole thing with fine sewing cotton on the outside. Make the ears in the same way as the body and fold them before stitching in position. The mane is two layers of fringed red felt and the tail a thick roll of the same. Cut the saddle from paper and try it over the back. Remember to allow enough to go over the back gusset. Cover the paper with black fabric and embroider it in white. Hem the saddle on with matching thread; also a strip for the girth.

The last horse of these three (page 54) is made from white corded taffeta—a lovely rich fabric—and worked with two strands of stranded cotton in red, jade green, bright yellow and black. The central stalks are black chain, the short branches black fly. The flowers red chain with a solid green centre and yellow branches. Yellow buttonhole and red chain for the feet. The triangles along the back are outlined with black buttonhole, then inner lines of red and yellow chain, with the centre filled with green French knots. The underbody has green stars of straight stitch and red French knots scattered about. Make the animal in the same way as the cotton one.

The saddle is yellow taffeta worked with black and red. The harness could be a fine red cord or a black band with yellow stitching, or a strip of green felt cut with pinking shears. For the mane and tail make a fringe of white rayon cord. Stitch it on first, then cut and unravel it. It makes a rich, light, fluffy and decorative finish.

A tiny pommel may be added to the saddle. Stitch two small rectangles of fabric together, turning in the edges right round. Then roll tightly into a tube, stitch down the edge and sew to the front of the saddle. Further decoration may be added after the tube has been sewn up.

A COLT

Page 56 shows a lively little horse full of verve and action. He is made on the same principle as the previous three but is a little more complicated in shape. The fabric for the sides is a fairly broad yellow and white stripe, mounted on a paper shape of course. All the stitchery is in grey and some use is made of the stripes. Fly stitch for the legs and down the body. Fly and knots of chain along the main body stripe with French knots filling in the spaces. The back gusset is light grey fabric with a woven diamond in it. These are enriched by a row of darker grey running and a second row of lemon chain stitch. The underbody is plain dark grey material with a running stitch worked in thick white cotton.

Assemble and stuff the animal as described for the other horse. The ears are light grey material folded at the base before being stitched on, while the mane and tail are both fringes of thick black cotton. The tail is rather short and chunky and the mane is cut quite close after it has been stitched on.

CAT

For the cat lovers there is an amusing sitting cat and a tiger which could be adapted to a leopard, panther, lion, puma or any member of the feline species (pp. 58–9).

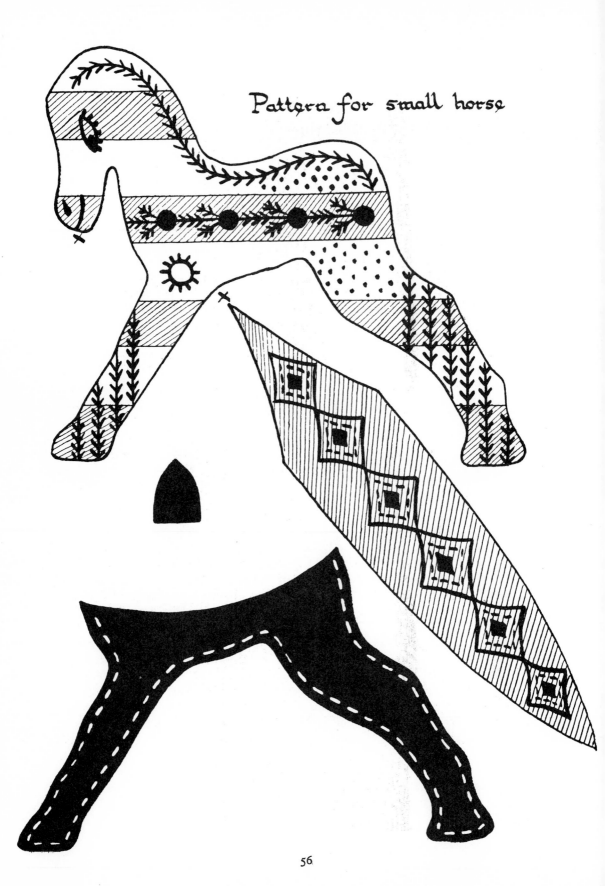

Pattern for small horse

PLATE 3

PLATE 4

The sitting cat consists of two side shapes, including the head, which faces sideways, and two underbody sections. It is fun to make this cat from striped, checked or spotted fabric, adding a very little stitching to the pattern on the material. A couched thread along all the seams improves it too. Use the same pattern for the body for the cat with the separate head, cutting it off at the neck. The head has two side sections and one V-shaped front gusset. The point of this fits in at the nose. The back of the head has two pieces joined together down the centre along the curved edges. This is then sewn on to the front. Stuff the body and the head separately. You will probably have to stuff the tail from the end and sew up the seam afterwards. Sew the head on to the neck and then cut two ears from felt and attach them to the top of the head in an upright position. A narrow collar makes a good finish for the neck. Embroider the eyes, nose and whiskers after the animal has been stuffed. You might like to make a family of cats using differently patterned fabrics of the same colours. For instance black and white plain, striped and checked materials combined in several ways, having different ones for head, undergusset and body.

TIGER

The tiger is a larger animal with its feet in a walking position. All the sections have a paper base. Do be careful when cutting the undergussets to see that they match with their appropriate side pieces, as they are both different. All the seams are sewn on the outside with fine cotton. The original is made from yellow and black striped taffeta for the body with cream flannel for the undergusset. The black stripes are emphasized with extra black fly stitch in a thick cotton with thinner chain stitch stripes in between. The back gusset starts under the chin and finishes at the tail. In the diagram you will find it in two pieces but when you cut your pattern make it in one continuous strip. If you are using striped fabric it is as well to try and make the gusset stripes fit with those on the side when they meet to form the back.

For the tail, cover two pipe-cleaners with a tube of the striped fabric. It may then be bent into position. Make the eyes with green chain and green sequins. The whiskers are pieces of wire threaded through the head after the animal has been stuffed. Cut the ears from black felt and sew them on in a folded position.

LIZARD

The lizard (page 60) is an example of a flat crawling animal. Make your side view drawing as for the others, but instead of having a curved line at the top of the underbody make it perfectly straight. Place this line to a fold when cutting out the undergusset so that you have it all in one piece. A small gusset improves the shape of the head.

This animal is made from bright blue felt for the sides with a lime green underbody. A sharp contrast in colour adds interest and excitement. Work with two strands of stranded cotton. The loops are orange chain with a lime detached chain inside. The circles solid knobs of white chain. The zig-zag line along the back is lime buttonhole with a second line of orange coral knot, while the leaf shapes are white detached chain. Work the lines on the legs in lime stem stitch and the toes with orange single fly. Lime running stitch along the jaws and orange chain for the mouth. Work this after the creature

Head Gusset

Head Back Cut 2

Head Side Piece

Under Gusset

Ear

Pattern for sitting cat
with separate head

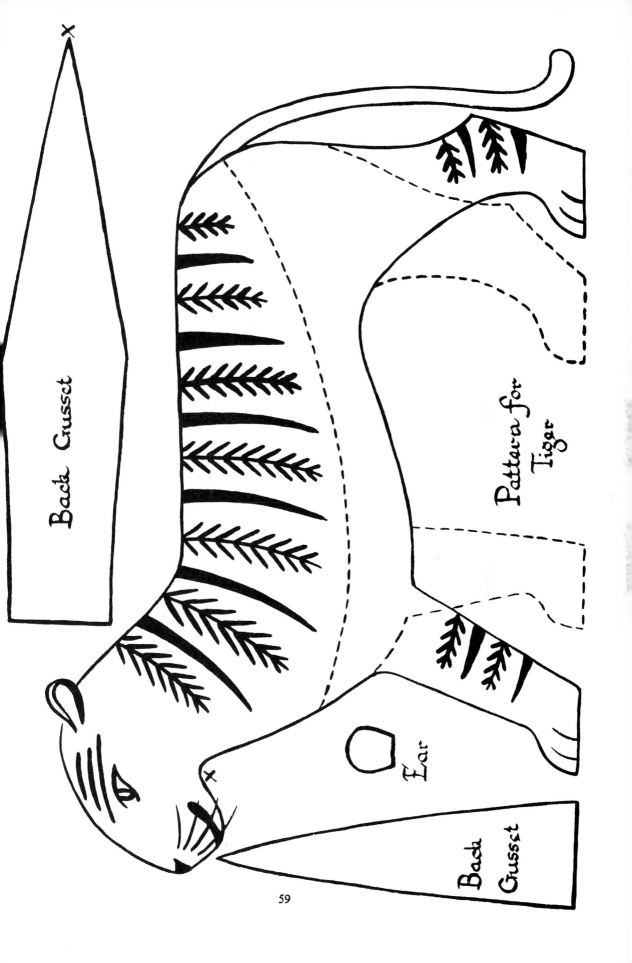

Back Gusset

Pattern for
Tiger

Ear

Back
Gusset

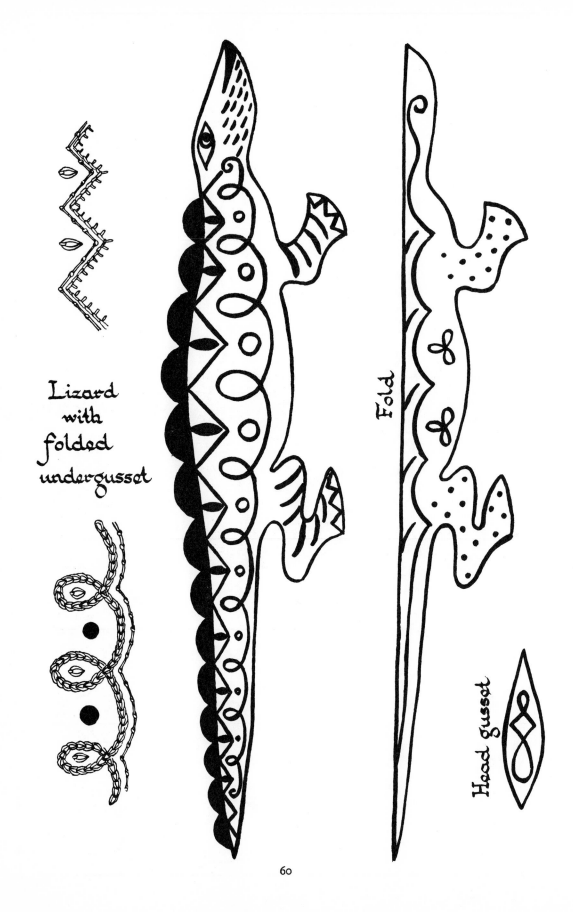

Lizard
with
folded
undergusset

Fold

Head gusset

has been assembled and stuffed. Underneath the main scalloped line is orange chain with blue branches of fly stitch and detached chain down the middle. Three blue detached chain make the shamrock shapes and orange French knots decorate the legs.

Seam the pieces together on the right side with two strands of stranded cotton. A crest along the back is an attractive addition. Cut this from a single strip of felt—scalloped or vandyked along the edge—and stitch it in when sewing the back sections together. The scallops look better if they are graduated in size—bigger in the middle and smaller towards head and tail. A gusset could be added round the mouth—use a different colour to suggest the inside of the mouth and embroider teeth along the edge.

TOAD

The toad (page 62) is made in the same way as the lizard with a folded gusset for the underbody. It is much wider, giving a chunkier-looking animal. There is also a broad back gusset to give the flat back of the toad. This animal is enriched with beads, sequins and jewels as well as a little embroidery.

Use dark green felt for the sides and back gusset. This has large oval-shaped pearly sequins with small dark green ones stitched on with gold beads in between. The sides have lines of white chain. Long scarlet beads sloping along the top edge, dark green sequins attached with red beads in the next space, long white glass beads next and bronze sequins sewn on with gold beads along the bottom. Red buttonhole is worked along the line of the leg and red coral knot for the toes. The back legs have biggish white glass beads scattered on them. The prominent glittering eye is made with a central diamanté jewel surrounded by bronze beads, red chain stitch and finally a circle of white beads. Work the mouth with red chain stitch. For the bright underbody—in contrast with the dark back—use lemon felt. Down the centre sew on large bright green sequins and spatter tiny red glass beads on the legs and chin. This toad would look beautiful if made in a rich silk or taffeta. He could really be the one that changed into the prince in the fairytale. The whole creature is assembled with fishbone stitch in a fine lemon cotton.

GRIFFIN*

In the griffin (pages 64–5) we have an example of a walking animal. Each side must be drawn separately with legs in the correct position. When you have done this put the two shapes together and see if they fit and look right. The feet must be level. Sometimes one leg may be raised, but make certain that the animal will stand on three legs. The two underbody sections must match their respective side pieces.

The griffin is made in several coloured felts, pink, green, white and navy. Cut one side in green felt and one in pink. The legs have applied pieces of navy blue felt—scalloped on the back legs and vandyked on the front. Hem these pieces on first. Then transfer the design on to the felt and work it with two strands of embroidery cotton. On the pink side the neck is scalloped in the form of scales. These are worked with white chain, a second line of navy chain just inside, and a green star in the middle of each scallop. At the top of each is a white tête-de-bœuf stitch.

The body consists of lines of green chain with navy single fly and grey detached chain along one side, and white feather stitch along the other. The front leg has white fly stitch

*See also illustration facing p. 128.

Toad decorated with beads and sequins

Fold

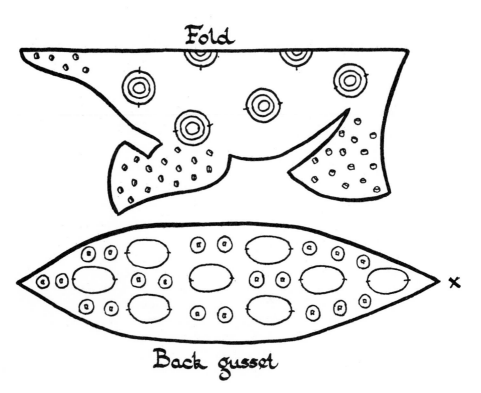

Back gusset

on each pointed piece of the navy appliqué, with detached chain and fly in the spaces. The back leg has the navy appliqué covered with green French knots with a surrounding edge of white coral knot. This is continued in the scalloped line with fly stitch at the points.

The green side of the body is the same with pink thread in place of the green. The legs are slightly different. On the front one work a green detached chain and fly on the navy vandyke with white fly stitches in the spaces. On the back embroider a line of pink fly down the straight side of the navy appliqué, pink coral knot along the scalloped edge, pink stars in the spaces. White coral follows the scalloped line of the navy felt a short distance from the edge.

The underbody is cut from white felt and left plain. Cut the back gusset from white too. Notice that it goes right round the nose into the mouth and out again, ending at the front of the lower jaw. This gives an open mouth. The back gusset has a central line of pink chain, green buttonhole diamonds, grey detached chain and fly and navy spots of solid chain. Navy single fly on each side of the line comes along the top of the face. Work a line of navy coral knot round the mouth and work the eye in navy and white. Sew all the pieces together with white fishbone stitch, remembering that the back gusset starts at the front of the lower jaw and finishes at the tail. Be careful not to get this gusset twisted.

The legs, being so slender, need to be wired. If you find them difficult to stuff from the body, stuff about half-way up from the foot end, sewing in the tiny soles of navy felt afterwards. Then continue stuffing as for the other animals. Cut a piece of pink felt for the tongue and stitch to the back of the mouth. Bind a length of millinery wire with green thread for the tail—about 5"—and make a fringed white felt roll for the end. The ears are cut from navy felt and stitched on in a V position.

Now make the wings from white felt—two pieces for each wing. The outer side is elaborately worked with dividing lines of navy feather stitch and leaf shapes of pink chain filled with green herringbone. The outer edge has pink vandyke buttonhole, and French knots are worked in all the spaces. The underwing has three small spokes of green fly at the base and four rows of equally spaced running stitch following the line of the scalloped edge. Place a piece of tailor's canvas between the two sides of each wing and stitch them together with white fishbone. Attach them to the animal's back in a slight curve towards the centre of it.

Although the griffin seems difficult to make he is a lovely piece of decoration. If you are accurate with the cutting and careful with the assembling and wiring, you will have no trouble. One could even add felt teeth—cut with the pinking shears. Sew them into the jaw edges when stitching together.

A really delightful idea is to make families of animals. You could have mother horse with a foal—rather like her but not quite the same, or mother lizard with a trail of babies.

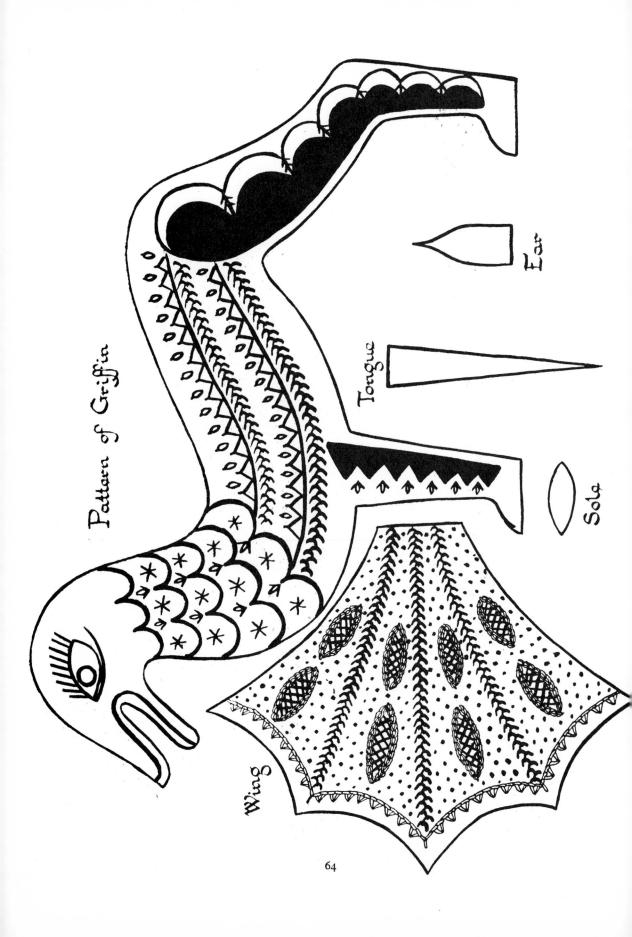

Pattern of Griffin

Ear

Tongue

Sole

Wing

64

Head and back gusset

Section Four

BIRDS

O F ALL KINDS OF FOLK TOYS, bird shapes are the most popular. They originated in the form of a whistle and were given as gifts at Easter time. Indeed they still are. Birds have the most wonderful colours and plumage and so they provide great scope for creating creatures of fantasy. One can use rich fabrics and make gorgeous imaginative crests and tails. On the whole the bird shape itself is basically simple, but with the addition of gay appendages one can transform it into a creature of splendour.

BEAKS

On page 67 you will find several ways of making beaks. No doubt you will be able to add to these when you come to consider the bird you are making.

A flat beak is made on a hairpin base. Bind the curved end with thread and then weave it under one side and over the other, keeping the threads close together until you have filled in all the spaces. Two such hairpins make a flat beak. Pierce the head of the bird with the ends of the wire and sew them into place with a few invisible stitches.

A fabric beak can be made with two triangles of paper covered with material. After folding over the edges and tacking them, seam together on the outside. Stuff from the top and then hem on to the bird.

A similar beak is made from felt, stitched with fishbone, stuffed and sewn on with the stitching at the sides instead of top and bottom as with the previous one.

The fourth beak is made from four pieces of felt or fabric. Each pair is sewn together and a slightly smaller piece of card the same shape is slipped inside each. Slightly pad on one side of the card—giving a flat side and a round one. Sew them on to the bird with flat sides facing. This beak would look attractive in two colours, one outside and one inside.

HEADS AND CRESTS

Crests are an important part of the bird. You can really let your imagination run riot with them. On pages 69–71 I have included some suggestions for birds' heads. You may want to make them and attach a suitable body, or they may inspire you to create something of your own. First we have a head and beak cut in one with rows of back-stitch to suggest the bill. The eye could be a curtain ring stitched on at intervals with oversewing; French knots are added over the head. The crest is two rounded pieces of fabric with couched loops worked on the outside of each. These are sewn together and inserted as the head is put together. Running stitch, vandyked felt and threaded running decorate the neck. Other braids would look equally well—a small ric-rac for instance.

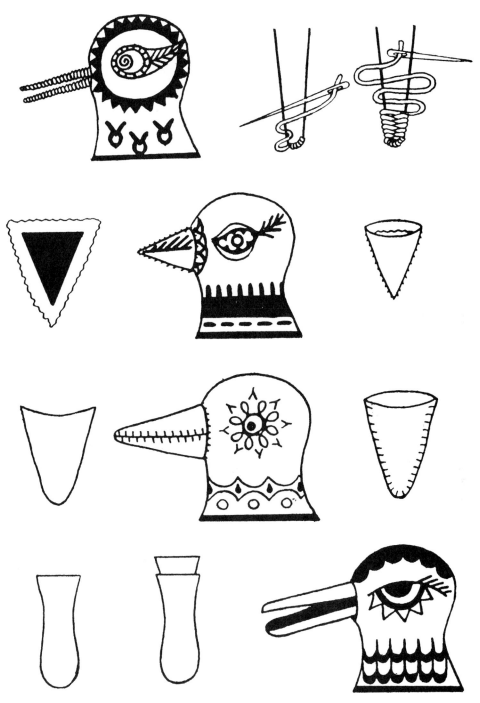

Some beaks and bird heads

We next have a bird with a hairpin beak and loops of stiffish ribbon for the crest. Sew these in as you stitch the head together. The eye is satin stitch encircled with backstitch, with buttonhole at the front and straight stitches like spokes at the back. Round the head is single fly stitch. The neck has two rows of scalloped buttonhole with detached chain and fly in the top scallops, and branches of fly stitch extending downwards from the bottom ones.

The third head is made from two different fabrics. Cut each piece in paper and cover with the appropriate material, plain for the head, stripy for the neck. Seam them together carefully on the wrong side. Decorate the stripes with continuous chain and fly and solid spots of chain in alternate stripes. Feather stitch emphasizes the curve of the head. Long narrow single fly stitches with straight stitch in the spaces surround the eye. The crest is three curved feathers set at suitable intervals.

Then again we have two felts for the next bird. These are cut in a vandyke shape to fit in to each other and put together with fishbone. Loops of couching fit into the zig-zags above and below the join. Detached chain goes round the head and the eye is a combination of coral, stem and buttonhole. For the crest cut a single piece of felt and work an even running stitch along the edge. See that it is straight on both sides. Then work a saddle stitch and finish it off by threading with a second colour, thus making a row of pekinese. Do this on both sides and insert the crest when sewing up the head. A line of buttonhole along the beak is a little further decoration. Number 5 (page 70) is a slender delicate head with a fine looped design round it. The beak would be cut in two or four sections for the curved and pointed effect. The crest is a bunch of stamens. You can buy these in a wonderful assortment of shapes and in all colours—from tiny stamen heads like a pin, to lovely glittering jewels and smooth pearls. Embroider the neck with herringbone and attach the circular collar after the bird has been stuffed.

Next there is a heavier-looking bird, with a large beak. Make this in two sections and add the embroidery when they are sewn together. The crest is cut in felt points which slope back over the head. A bold coil winds round the head, leading to the eye. Small felt shapes are applied to the neck. Buttonhole stitch is added to them.

The crest of the next bird is two paper shapes covered with thin fabric. Embroider each one with feather stitch and chain, then stitch them together on the right side. Insert the crest in the top of the head when assembling the bird. The eye is a circle of felt cut on the outside with pinking shears. There is a hole in the centre. Stitch it on with long straight stitches from the hole to the inside corners of the zig-zags. An additional piece is sewn in below the striped beak—made in the same way as the crest. The embroidered neck has various kinds of chain stitches, vandyke buttonhole and couching.

The last bird on this page has the beak cut in one with the body. It is elaborated with beads, as is the neck. Here we have two colours between wavy lines of chain stitch. The eye is a large sequin surrounded by medium-sized beads, then single fly stitch with tiny beads. For the crest it has short pieces of feather—perhaps ends you have cut off the curved ones used for the bird on page 69.

A lovely crest could be a series of small pom-poms stitched on to fine wires and grouped together at the top of the head (page 71). You could bind or paint the wires. The curved beak should be made in two or four sections sewn with fishbone.

Bird heads and crests

69

More bird heads and crests

Crests

One large pom-pom makes another crest.   Stitch it firmly to the head and then clip to shape and size with very sharp scissors.   It should not appear raggy.

Next we have a patchwork crest.   Each section is cut in paper first, then covered with fabric and the whole stitched together on the wrong side, fine seaming.   Stuff from the bottom and then stitch on the head.

The next kind has the crest in one with the body and beak.   The embroidery suggests it—rows of running stitches.   A back gusset starting with a point at the top of the crest and widening out along the back would improve this shape.

Then there is another felt crest.   This comprises a series of felt shapes.   One large one for the centre, a smaller one on each side of it and a smaller one still on each side of these.   Use fine felt or it will be too bulky.   Contrasting colours or tones would be attractive.   The long thin beak would be better wired.

Finally there is a second stuffed crest.   Cut the two sides, embroider them, stitch together and stuff before stitching on to the bird.   A triangular gusset down the back edge would make a more solid crest.   This bird has thickish thread for the eye and very fine for the plumage round it.

BIRD TAILS

From heads to tails.   You can really let yourself go with birds' tails and make the most gorgeous and exotic creations.   You will find some suggestions and methods in the diagrams on pages 73 and 75, but do not stop at these.   Try to invent your own ways and creations.   You can use feathers of all kinds—even those stolen from the pillow or quilt.   A single curly feather, or two or three all of the same size or graduated, can make a handsome tail.   A feather cut to a different shape or even one cut off short as on page 73, second from top, looks attractive.   A short tail usually gives a pert look to the bird.

Then there are the felt shapes.   Vary them in size—something like a cockerel's tail —and after you have worked them stitch thin card between.   Work two sides for each tail piece, of course.   A large flat shape is good for elaborate embroidery.   That in the third diagram on page 73 shows quite a lot of decoration.   Again work this before making up the tail.   You could have each side a different colour.   The edge is a strip of pinked felt inserted between the two sides.   Another idea is to cover long finger shapes of card with embroidered fabric and stitch them round the tail.   Any number of these could be arranged—perhaps varying them in size—having the largest in the middle and the smaller ones towards the sides.   They could be embroidered to look like feathers. If the body of the bird is felt you could cut a slit and fix the tail feathers in that.   Then a single tail or feather shape cut in card and covered with elaborately embroidered material makes a lovely finish to a more formal bird.   This larger type of tail gives more scope for decoration and smaller patterns may be worked within the larger one.   Next there is the downward sweeping tail—made on the same principle as the previous one.   The top should be shaped like a V so that it will fit round the body of the bird and stand off a little.   Once again a contrast both in stitch and fabric for the underside would be attractive.

Wire is useful for birds' tails.   It may be bent and twisted to form many shapes and often gives a more delicate finish to a bird than a solid tail of fabric.   Try two leaf shapes

Some ideas
for bird
tails

of felt as on page 75, top left. Sew them together with running stitch, inserting the wire down the divisions. The sewing on each side keeps it rigid once it has been fastened inside the bird. Finish off the wire ends with pom-poms, stuffed knobs of felt, fancy buttons, discs of fabric or anything appropriate. You can also bind or paint the wire.

A similar tail is made with several separate pieces of wire bound with thread, each having an embroidered leaf shape on the end. Cut the shapes in paper, cover them with fabric, decorate them with stitching or beads and sew the two sides together with the wire in between. When fastening the wires to the bird stitch each one in separately so that they retain their position and do not fall about. You could have them as in the diagram or pointing downwards, upwards or both.

Attractive, delicate tails may be fashioned with wire and beads. You could have three loops of threaded beads twisted together at the bottom and a single line with a glittering jewel at the top for the centre. To make this tail fairly rigid thread one loop first and secure at the bottom by twisting. Tie on your second piece of wire. Then thread about a third of the beads on to the second wire and twist this between two beads of the first loop about a third of the way along. Finish threading your second loop and twist the end of the wire to that of the first. Repeat with the third loop. They will all stay in position as one piece. Most jewels have a hole pierced—slip the wire through and bring the short end down by the side of the long one. Now thread on your beads over both wires. Twist the end round the others.

A second wire tail consists of tiny beads and star-shaped sequins. Slip a bead on to a piece of fine wire, bend the end over—making it lie by the side of the long piece— the bead is right in the bend. Then thread on your sequins and beads in any sequence you wish—threading over both strands of wire until the short one disappears. Make any number of these tail " feathers " and twist them all together at the bottom. The twisted ends of course are fastened inside the bird.

Downward sweeping feathers give a lovely tail if you can manage to cut them to give the right sweeping effect. On the other hand felt supported by pliable wire may be bent how you please. Cut the tail shapes from felt. Fold each in half lengthways over a piece of wire and work a line of close running or backstitch underneath—sufficient to hold the wire in position. Another way would be to have two felt shapes for each tail piece. Place the wire down the centre between each pair of shapes and work a running along each side of it—right through both pieces of felt. The running could be elaborated with other colours if you wished. Or the top piece of felt could be dark and the under piece light. There are many variations. Stitch round the edges of the felt after fixing the wire.

Finally, a fringe stiffened with wire along the top makes an elaborate tail. Make a fringe as described for making a fringed mane, but before removing the threads from the piece of card, firmly sew a length of wire along the top. Cut the threads at the bottom and remove the card. The wire may be left at the top or the fringe turned over. You can bend it into any position.

BIRD WINGS

Wings are an essential addition to the bird. One may work wing shapes directly

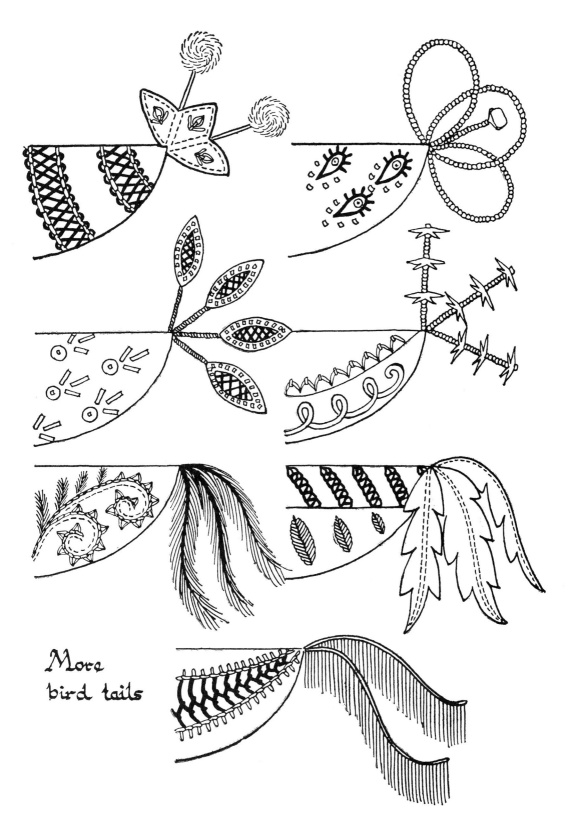

More
bird tails

75

on to the body or make, embroider and attach them separately.   If you are using felt or leather the wing could be just one thickness, but all other fabrics will need a lining.   Quite free embroidery or stitches suggesting the plumage are all suitable.   One can find a great deal of inspiration from looking at the actual bird or its photograph.   The feathers, whether they are tiny round ones in scale-like layers, or long sweeping ones, may all be translated into embroidery.   See that the shape of the wing itself is in keeping with the bird.   If they are too big and heavy the bird looks unbalanced and clumsy.   If too small they do not fit in with the general design and look as if they have been stuck on as an after-thought.   Always draw in the wing when making the pattern, even though it will be a separate item.   Before you attach the wing try it in several positions until you arrive at the right one.

In the first design on page 77 you can see a very simple wing decorated with a continuous line of running winding into the centre.   Two sides are stitched together with fishbone.   Have a different stitch on the other piece, spots, circles, stars or anything simple to correspond with the running stitch.

Next there is a wing with a straight edge.   This is made in a finer fabric and seamed on the right side.

The next wing is rather more complicated.   It is made in layers of three separate colours and fabrics.   Make each piece separately.   The large bottom section is the full wing shape with the smaller ones placed on top of it.   Each section is of double fabric. You can make them in felt—this is easiest—or in finer materials by tacking over paper shapes or by sewing on the wrong side and turning out.   If you use this method be sure to clip right down into the corners of the scallops.   Then there will be no dragging. As well as several colours, different textures might look well. For instance, velvet for the two small sections and fine wool for the large one.

Again there is another simple wing.   The circular embroidery suggests the small compact plumage at the front of the wing, while the lines of running suggest the longer feathers.

A similar idea is carried out in the long wing.   It has not such a smooth line—the scallops following the line of the feathers.

A patchwork wing is made in felt by stitching the sections with fishbone.   If this same one is assembled in other material, seam the pieces together on the wrong side after first mounting on paper.   Do not forget to line the wing.   A contrast in stitching looks attractive too.   Work straight stitch stars on the round section and alternating rows of single fly and buttonhole on the other.

Two wing sections stitched together with a fancy felt edge in between is another decoration (page 78).   The felt edge could be cut into all manner of shapes and it could extend round three sides of the wing if necessary.

A second wing in layers may be cut in felt.   Try varying the edges of each section as well as the colours.   Cut the largest piece first and fit the others on it in paper before cutting the fabric.   Stitch them all together at the top edge.

Work out some-time a patchwork wing made from plain and patterned fabrics. Mount each piece on paper, perhaps with the patterned material between two plain sections.   Seam them together on the wrong side and then embroider.   If your material

Bird wings

More wings

is very fine have thin delicate embroidery—perhaps worked in sewing cotton. The whole shape could be lined with one large wing section as a contrast to the patchwork.

The fourth wing on this page is a more complicated patchwork one. All the sections must be cut accurately or they will not fit together. The whole wing is fitted into a little cup of felt at the top. Various stitches are used to suggest the grain of the wing feathers.

Then there is a simple wing shape made from striped fabric with bands of plain, either applied over it or inserted between as for a patchwork wing. Suitable embroidery may be carried out along the plain strips and/or down the stripes.

You might try a wing made of layers of strongly contrasting materials—perhaps felt and fine cotton. That in the diagram shows a basic shape covered with spotted cotton, then two rounded pieces of felt cut with the pinking shears, next two smaller cotton shapes and finally all these enclosed in a small cup of felt. This type of wing would need to be lined.

BIRD FEET AND STANDS

Quite a number of bird patterns are for a standing bird, so I would like to mention one or two ways of making feet or stands. A bird looks most attractive on a solid base, and it can be decorated in keeping with the animal. The easiest base to make is a round tube. Cut a circle for the base and a strip long enough to go round it. Embroider it, stitch the strip ends together and sew this on to the circular base. Sometimes it is wise to put a weight in the bottom, a small lead button, as well as a piece of stiff card, so that there is a flat base for the tube to stand on. Then stuff it to keep its shape and stitch to the underneath of the bird.

A cone makes a substantial stand and is made in the same way as the tube. The side piece of course must be drawn out correctly first. Do not make the top too narrow or the bird will wobble about. Square or oblong stands could be devised too.

A progression of the cone or tube is to cover a cotton reel. Those with the sloping ends top and bottom are the best. Cut paper shapes to fit each section of the reel before you make them in fabric and work the embroidery before you stitch the sections round the bobbin.

A firm stuffed leg (top left) is made by cutting two pieces of fabric the length of the leg plus half the length of the foot—all in one piece. They may be graduated—thicker at the top of the leg but not *too* narrow at the ankle or foot, otherwise the bird will not stand. Do not have the strips too thin—wide enough to make a nice rounded leg when stitched together and stuffed. Drawing paper used as a base makes these legs more substantial. Work the embroidery on each piece, then sew them together down the sides until you reach the foot section. Leave this open and fold one piece forward and the other backwards. Put a piece of firm card underneath cut to size and then a piece of felt or fabric. Stitch this small piece of material to the sections you folded fore and aft. The card makes a flat stand. Gently stuff the leg from the open end and then stitch the top to the bird. Do see that the legs are in the right position for the bird to stand well. If they are not correct the body will overbalance, so it is as well to spend some time trying the legs in different positions until you find the most satisfactory. This applies to all legs and stands.

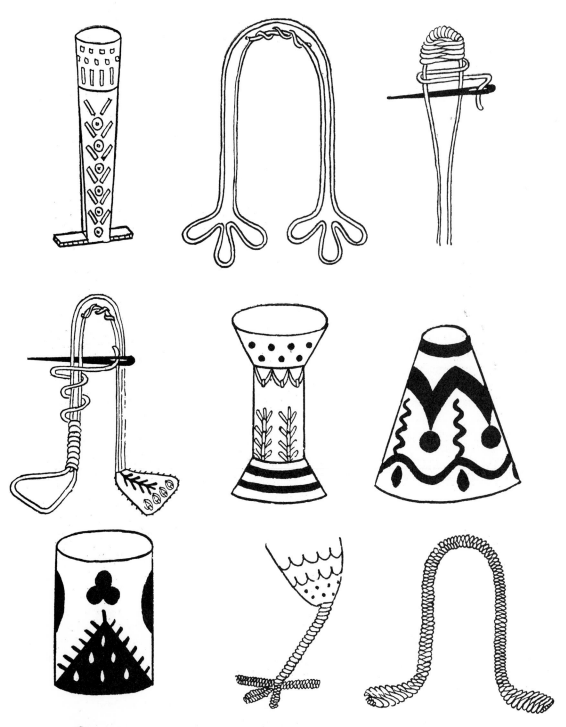

Some ways of making bird legs

Wire legs are perhaps the most difficult.   I find the best way is to bend the wire as in the diagram.   Start in the middle, come down to the foot making two or three claws, back over the middle to the second foot, and then back to the beginning.   Twist the two ends together.   The wire frame can be covered with two pieces of felt cut to the right size and shape and stitched carefully together with the wire in between.

Or you could cover the wires with thread.   This is done in the same way as you covered the hairpin beak.   Bind the thread round the curved end first.   Then weave it under and over the wires until the foot is covered in.   Then either continue to weave the thread between the two wires for the legs *or* bind it tightly round them.   If you have more than one claw on the foot, start in the same way at the end of one spur and continue up round the leg wires, finishing at the end of a spur on the other foot.   Then work in the remaining claws separately, fastening off invisibly.

When you are sewing up the bird leave enough space open at each side of the body to slide the legs and feet through.   Push one half through and bend into position.   Stuff the bird, and when you have decided on the correct place for the leg wires sew up the opening in the body and at the same time catch in the thread on the legs so that they are quite secure.   You can still bend them about a little until they are quite right.   A beginner might find it easier to stitch the wire legs on to the outside of the bird after it has been stuffed.

Another alternative is to bind only the leg part of the wires and to cover the feet with fabric which fits round the wire shape of the foot.   You could make each leg separately and pad the top half—cutting two shapes of fabric, wide at the top and narrowing to fit the wire leg at a point not quite half-way down (centre drawing, bottom row).   Sew the material on to the bound wire leg at this point and then stuff inside the fabric.   The top of this pad would then be sewn on to the bird body.

Try covering wires with different kinds of thread.   It is surprising what a variety of effects you can create.   Thick soft cotton, metallic thread, bobbly yarn, fine embroidery silk are all suitable.   Do see that the legs or stand are in proportion to the bird and that they are set so that the bird is properly balanced.

The same rules apply for bird patterns as for animal ones.   Keep the shape simple and without fussiness.   Elaborate decoration is better added in the form of crests, tails, etc.   There is more scope for embroidery on a good bold shape, and a smooth unbroken outline is very satisfactory to the eye.

SITTING BIRD—HEN

The easiest bird to make is the sitting one—a hen or duck.   This consists of two side shapes embracing the whole of the body, beak included if you wish—although in the diagram (page 82) I have put in a separate beak, and a long gusset which stretches from the tail to just under the beak.   This is tapered at each end with the broadest, flattest section in the middle—just where the animal will sit.   The pattern I have given is for a mother hen—made in different coloured felts.   Cut each piece and embroider it before assembling.

The head and neck is of lemon felt divided by a zig-zag line from a black body.   You could cut the whole section in one piece if you liked.   If you have two colours sew them

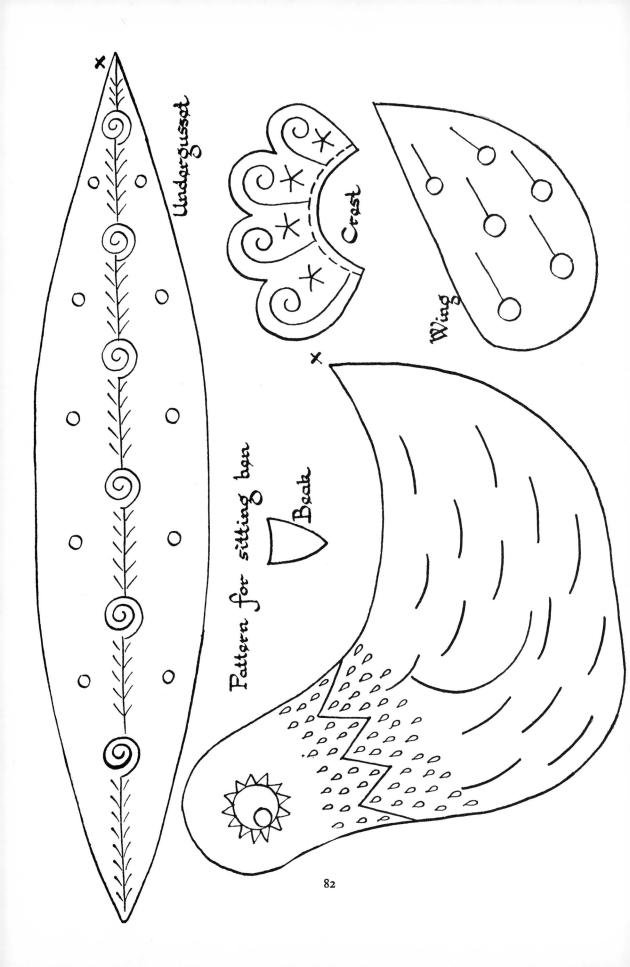

Undergusset

Crest

Wing

Beak

Pattern for sitting hen

together with lemon fishbone. Work black detached chain on the lemon felt and red on the black. The body has branches of white fly stitch. The eye is black chain and green vandyke buttonhole and the line down the head red feather stitch. Make the wings of lemon worked with black spots of chain with tails of green fly. Line them with white felt that has a continuous line of red running stitch round it.

The gusset is white. It has a central green fly stitch, spots of solid red chain and whirls of black running. Use double red felt for the crest, decorating each side with black stars and curls of white coral knot. Stitch the two sides of the crest together with matching thread. Sew the bird with white fishbone stitch, including the crest as you come to it. The gusset fits from the tail to just below the beak. Stuff firmly. Sew the outer wings and lining together and attach to the hen. Sew two sides of the beak, stuff and stitch in position.

This bird looks even better if she has a nest to sit on. You could easily make one of yellow raffia. Take several strands together and loosely sew them into a nest. Start at the bottom and wind them round into an oval shape, then build a little up the sides. You could even make some embroidered eggs ! French knots, bands of chain or branches of fly stitch would be appropriate decoration for them.

SECTIONAL BIRD

Why not try a bird made like those cut from sections of wood ? Sometimes they had a flat circle for a head, a tube for a neck, another for the body and a third to stand on. Or it might be made from a potato, small for the head, large for the body with a feather for a tail. It might even have a fir cone for the body, feather for a tail and small potato for the head. I have included a sectional bird built on the fir cone principle (page 84). Two large shapes for the body, two small similar pieces for the head. Decorate them—perhaps with appliqué and very little embroidery—stuff, and stitch the head into position. A feather from the pillow would look well for the tail. A stand could be made from a flat round tube. Draw round a halfpenny for the base and a $\frac{1}{2}''$ wide strip round this. Put a circle of firm card in the base, stuff and stitch to the bird. You could add wings if you wanted to make it more elaborate. A fatter bird would result from stitching a continuous strip round the body and head sections as described for the dachshund.

THREE BIRDS ON CONICAL STANDS

I have shown three small birds and how one can develop the original shape by the addition of various appendages (page 85). All these birds are made of fine woollen fabric so that all the shapes must be cut first in paper. Head, body and beak are all in one piece. There is a long under gusset from chin to tail. The first bird is made in bright yellow with a line of dark blue fly stitch and white detached chain on the body. The eye is blue chain and white buttonhole. A circle of white running goes round the head. On the gusset work a line of blue feather stitch with white single fly on each side.

The birds all stand on cones. This one is in yellow to match the bird. Work a blue star on the base of the cone. Round the sides embroider a line of blue chain and a line of blue single fly. Work white detached chain in the spaces and white French knots

Bird shapes
based on potato
and cone birds

Small standing bird

in the space above. Stitch the pieces together with yellow thread and stuff firmly. Do not forget a piece of card in the base of the cone.

The second bird has the same stitching worked in different colours. The background fabric is grey woollen material with red, black and white stitching. The wings are made separately from red wool and decorated with white stitching. Do not forget to line them. They are attached after the bird has been stuffed.

The third member of this family has a red body worked with black and white, standing on a grey cone with red, black and white stitching. The wings and tail piece are grey also embroidered in red and white. The beak is separate, stuffed and stitched on when the body is finished. It and the crest are both yellow. Work the crest with black fly stitch. More elaborate tails and crests could be used instead of those in the diagram, or you might have a different stand—a tube or cotton reel.

LARGE DUCK

The pattern on pages 88–9 is for a large duck. Draw out squares twice the size of those in the diagram and re-draw the pattern. It makes a big bird. It is a good plan to make an outer cover over a stuffed shape of thin fabric. Then the cover can be removed and washed.

This pattern has two gussets, one underneath and one along the back from the tail to the top of the head. Cut the pattern in a reddish brown Viyella, leaving $\frac{1}{2}''$ turnings all round. Work all the embroidery in thick soft cotton. The tail feathers are navy fly stitch, the speckles light turquoise buttonhole with a large detached chain in the centre in darker turquoise. The top ring of the collar has dark turquoise coral knot on each side of light turquoise herringbone. The bottom ring is dark turquoise buttonhole on each side of dark cerise crested chain. Between the two is navy detached chain. The eye has white chain for the pupil with two rows of grey stem stitch round it. The outer circle is navy buttonhole and the half-circle yellow vandyke buttonhole.

Machine the pieces together on the wrong side, leaving a large enough opening along one of the bottom seams to push in the stuffed shape. Embroider the wings in scallops of navy buttonhole with white running above and lines of light turquoise fly stitch along the wing. Dark turquoise detached chain are scattered at the rounded end of the wing. The underside has grey running stitch. Sew the wing pieces together on the wrong side, with a layer of tailor's canvas to give them more body if you wish, leaving an opening to turn them out. Slip-stitch this together invisibly on the right side. Press all the pieces well and stitch the wings in position. Cut the crest and beak in yellow felt. Stitch the crest on with the points sloping backwards. Sew the beak together, stuff firmly and stitch in position. Make up another duck (without wings, crest or beak) in fine cotton material and stuff it well. Pull the embroidered cover over it and slip-stitch the opening. This may be unpicked when the outside has to be laundered.

COCKEREL

We now come to a bird with a cotton reel stand (page 87). He is a cockerel and a companion to the hen I described earlier. Make him in coloured felts. The body is divided into three, dark red for the main part, green for the head and a zig-zag white

Shapes for a standing cockerel

Beak

Crest

Wing

x

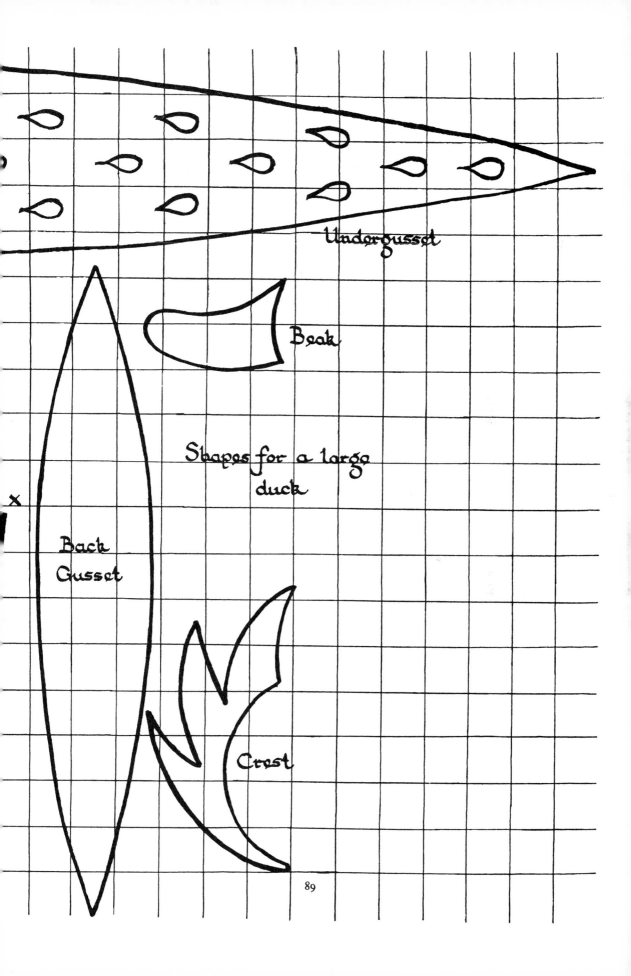

Undergusset

Beak

Shapes for a large
duck

Back
Gusset

x

Crest

89

band round the neck. Stitch these sections with fishbone. If you prefer it you can make the whole body in one colour.

Work the eye in black, white and red, the scallop in a double row of chain, pale mauve and jade green. The circles are spots of vivid red chain and the stars white. For the crest cut a single piece of scarlet felt. The gusset is lemon worked with dark red, black, jade green and scarlet. Cut the tail pieces in double felt, making the design on both sides, green for the largest, then mauve, and white for the smallest. Cut sections of card slightly smaller all round and seam them inside the two pieces of felt. Sew the animal with fishbone stitch, inserting the crest as you come to it. Stuff firmly, putting in the ends of the tail and stitching them into position so that they will not flap about. The wing pattern from the hen may be used, lemon outside and white underneath. Work a design on it to correspond with the body.

For the stand use a fattish cotton reel and cover it with felt, embroidering each piece first. Different colours look well—for instance jade for the top and bottom sections with white for the middle one. Finally sew the two beak sections together, stuff and sew in position.

TWO UPRIGHT BIRDS

We now come to a pattern where the stand is all in one with the body (page 91). This bird is tall, rather like the shape of an owl. It is made in felt with very simple stitching in two strands of stranded cotton and thick soft cotton. Cut the two side pieces in bright pink and work them with bands of white threaded running with grey fly stitch in between. Use the thinner thread for the fly stitch and running, threading it with the thick cotton. In all the spaces embroider thin black detached chain. Round the top of the head is thin black backstitch threaded with thick grey. The eye is a knob of fine black chain in a circle of white with a few detached chain springing from it.

Cut the front gusset from black felt. Work a line right round in thick and thin grey whipped running. The central space is filled with pink detached chain and fly. The lines of white chain at the bottom represent the feet. Sew the sections together with fine pink cotton. The point on the front gusset fits at the point on the underside of the beak. The small head gusset fits with the blunt end at the tip of the beak.

Stuff the bird from the bottom. Then stitch in the triangular base, first putting in a piece of strong card cut to the same shape. Cover all the seams with a thick grey thread couched with a fine cotton of the same colour. Sew on the black felt crest with the points sloping backwards.

Make the wings from grey felt outside and white inside. On the grey work a line of thin black running a little way from the outer edge. Inside this a line of pink whipped running. Run with thin thread and whip with thick. Then a curl of threaded backstitch. Backstitch with thin pink and thread with thick white. The two branches are thin black fly stitch. The white underwing has an outer line of thick pink running with five black stars in the space, worked with straight stitch in thin cotton. Seam the wing sections together with fine grey thread and then attach them for about $1\frac{1}{4}''$ along the top of the wing to the side of the bird.

The second standing bird (page 92), although made in the same way as the previous

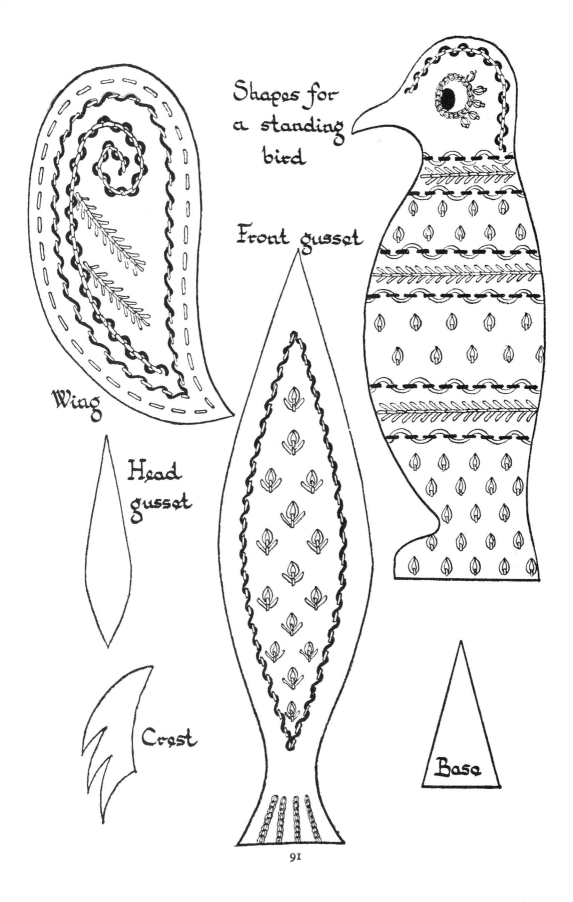

Wing

Shapes for a standing bird

Front gusset

Head gusset

Crest

Base

91

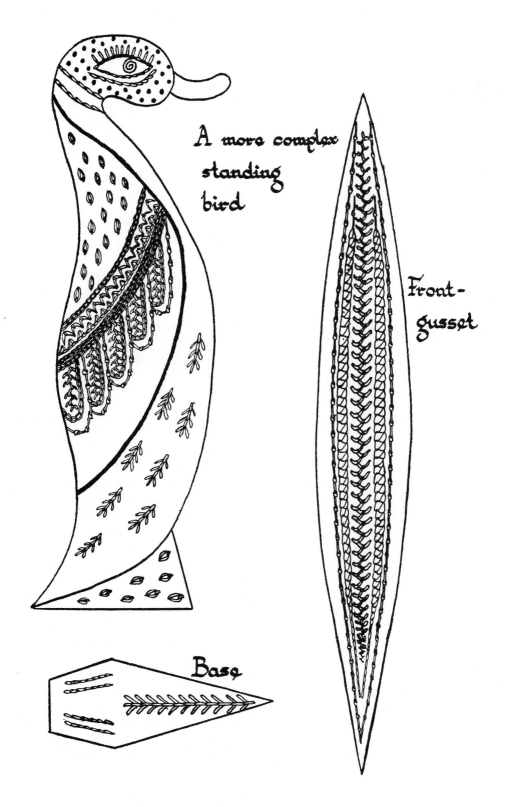

A more complex
standing
bird

Front-
gusset

Base

one, has finer and more complex stitchery. Cut the two side pieces in yellow and work black fly stitch branches at the bottom. Green French knots are on the head, with a black buttonhole and stem stitch for the eye round a knob of red chain. Two lines of red stem stitch are embroidered along the neck.

Cut two sections like those in the diagram bordered by the thick line. Use black felt for these. Work lemon detached chain at the top and then a border starting with green chain, lemon fly and chain, red vandyke buttonhole, green chain, lemon chain. The deep scallops are white coral knot with red chain and green feather inside them.

Make the front gusset from white felt having black feather stitch down the centre, green double chain on each side and red coral knot on each side of that. Stitch the gusset to the side pieces with fine thread. It stretches from the tail to just below the beak. Then sew round the head and down the beak. Sew the two black pieces along the back with matching cotton.

Make the stand from red felt. The triangular side pieces have black detached chain, the long piece has green fly stitch and black stem is used for the claws. Sew the long piece round the two sides of the triangles. Stuff the bird firmly and stitch up the opening. Put a piece of card in the base of the stand, stuff it and stitch to the bottom of the bird. Sew the black jacket over the yellow back. Stuff a red beak and sew it on. Cover all the seams with a thick white cotton couched in a fine white thread. This emphasizes the outline and gives a pleasing finish.

BIRD FAMILY

We now come to a little bird family—three sizes all built from the same pattern (page 94). Each bird is made from fabric that frays, so mount all the materials on paper shapes.

For the baby bird cut the sides from lemon taffeta and work the triangles with red buttonhole. The wing is worked directly on to the body with an outer line of dark blue chain and an inner one of grey coral knot. The collar is grey buttonhole with red herringbone underneath. The edge of the crest is red buttonhole and the beak lines of blue stem stitch. The gusset is a very narrow strip of grey and white silk with a line of dark blue coral knot and leaf shapes of red fly stitch. Make the legs of millinery wire, having two claws to each foot, and weave red silk round them. Sew up the bird with the legs in position and stuff, inserting a tiny curled feather for the tail.

Number two in the family has rather more elaborate embroidery. He is made in exactly the same way as the baby. The sides are of a rich blue taffeta with the wing worked on to the body. The stripes are white chain and dull green buttonhole, with pale pink herring-bone between. The long curved line is deep pink vandyke buttonhole. Navy blue detached chain is on the neck and rows of white running form the crest. The beak has rows of close pale pink buttonhole. Outline the wing with navy chain and the leaf shape with pink coral knot. Detached chain and fly in the dull green go down the centre. Make the gusset from white taffeta with spots of deep pink chain, stalks of dark blue fly and branches of black single feather stitch. Make the legs from wire with two claws to each foot, but bind them this time with navy thread. Stitch the bird together and stuff, adding a large white curled feather for the tail.

Patterns for
three birds of
different sizes

The largest member of the family is a beautiful creature. The body is white taffeta with quite elaborate embroidery. The V shapes have cerise buttonhole along the top edge and coral knot along the bottom. Inside are jade green detached chain stitches. The loop design is in black coral knot. Use chartreuse green for the eye and French knots on the beak with black vandyke buttonhole along the edges. The crest starts on the lower edge with jade chain followed by chartreuse chain, cerise French knots and black single fly.

For this bird the wings are made separately and stitched on after it has been stuffed. They are of cerise taffeta lined with white. On the cerise, work leaf shapes in jade buttonhole with white fly down the centre. The line running round the edge is black coral knot. Cut the gusset from cerise taffeta as well. The scallops are embroidered with white coral knot with a line of black running just inside. Work the drops down the centre in jade green with a single black chain inside each one. The legs are made separately of millinery wire bound with cerise thread from the ankle only. Cover the two claws of the feet with cerise material; one large triangle above and one below with the wire claws in between. Work two branches of jade fly stitch on the upper piece. Then stitch them together round the wire. Make a pad for the top of each leg from white taffeta. These are also triangular in shape—the widest part at the top. Sew them round the wire leg, stuff and embroider with cerise French knots. Then stitch the top of the pad to the bird's body. After stuffing the body add three large curled feathers for the tail, two green and one white.

Section Five

INSECTS AND FISH

BUTTERFLIES AND INSECTS make beautiful decorative toys. They are not as a rule suitable as playthings, but one can enjoy looking at them just as much as one might enjoy playing with some other toy. On the whole they are simple to assemble. Perhaps the very small insects are rather fiddling for young children. There is great scope for beads and sequins, delicate fabrics, laces and velvets, gold and silver thread.

INSECT WINGS

You will see some methods for the construction of wings in the diagram on page 97. Naturally they vary in shape, but that depends on the insect you are making. Unless the fabric is felt, mount all materials on paper, turning in the edges and tacking round. If the material is transparent, such as nylon, organdie, ninon or organza, be careful with the colour of the paper. Sometimes double fabric looks well. Of course the wings must be lined. The two layers of paper are sometimes stiff enough, but if a more rigid wing is required, put a thin piece of card or tailor's canvas in between the two layers of fabric.

You could also make a wire frame for the wing. Twist the wire into the correct shape, stretch the material over it and fasten down round the edge with running stitches just below the wire. Sew a lining over this, enclosing the wire inside two layers of material. You could then, if you wished, take out the running stitches.

A beaded wing could be made in the same way as described for the birds' tails. Various ways of joining the wires could be devised, scallops, loops, etc. If your fabric is soft and pliable, like nylon stocking material, it is a simple matter to stretch a piece over a very fine wire frame and gather it at the base. This could be bound with thread or covered with material or beads etc. when attached to the body.

LEGS AND FEELERS

Wire legs are made like those for the birds with binding or weaving. You may have different kinds of feet, or no feet at all, or just bend the wire into position. Stuffed knobs of fabric, discs, stuffed leaf shapes could all be used as feet. Feelers are made of wire too—perhaps decorated with knobs, jewels, sequins, etc.

SOME HINTS ON DESIGN

You can find a wealth of patterns by looking at pictures of butterflies and insects, or better still by studying the actual creatures. They have wonderful colours and designs on wing and body. The body shapes vary considerably ; some are long, slender, graceful, others short and stout, some hard, glittering and gleaming, others furry and velvety. Choose your fabrics to suggest the texture of the insect. Beware of very thick fabric ; if it is cut

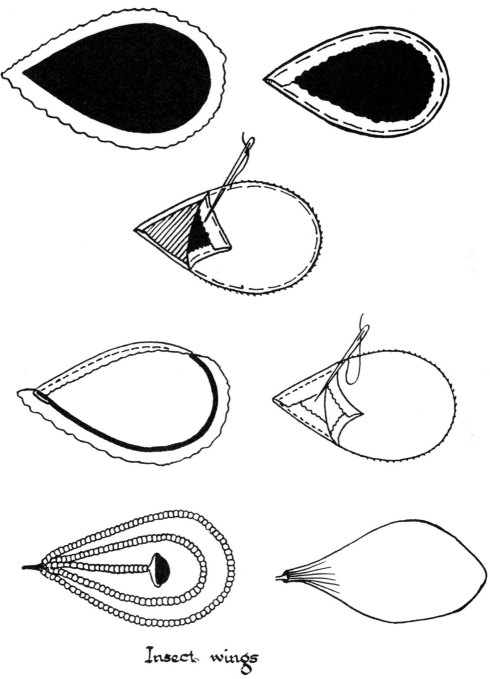

Insect wings

Butterfly Wings

into small shapes—with the exception of feet—it looks clumsy, and you will have difficulty in maintaining the original shape.

If the body is in sections, as it very often is, cut it all in one and suggest the divisions and colourings with embroidery. Very tiny pieces are difficult to stitch together satisfactorily. You can see on page 98 some suggestions for enriching wings and bodies with embroidery. Very often the use of thick and thin thread gives a pleasing texture, and of course beads and sequins make a wonderful decoration. As a rule the design on the natural butterfly has to be simplified for the embroidered one. Choose the main lines and circles and elaborate these with stitching if necessary. A gay bright upper wing contrasted with a more subdued underwing looks well, or a light delicate wing with a dark and gleaming body. No doubt other ideas will occur to you when you make a start on your insect. The patterns for the wings are just a flat outline. When making the pattern for the body draw the outline shape as if looking down on the creature. For the underbody halve the upper body shape exactly down the centre, then slightly curve the straight line outwards. When the two sections are stitched together for the underbody this curved line gives a roundness to it.

WASP OR FLY

The little wasp or fly (page 100) is very simple, but looks most attractive when finished. You will need only small scraps of material—but do be careful that the grain of the material goes the same way.

Cut all the shapes in drawing paper first. Cover the pieces for the upper wings with fine yellow fabric. On the two top ones work threaded backstitch with two strands of cotton, backstitch in grey, the threading in black round the edge. Then a line of grey coral knot. Branches of grey fly stitch are in the middle and four small gold sequins in the spaces. The lower wing has a circle of black buttonhole, a row of small bronze beads, a circle of grey coral knot and a gold sequin in the centre. The underwings are covered with grey nylon. Work a line of black coral knot round the upper pair. Then sew a bronze sequin and six long bronze beads in the centre. Small bronze beads are scattered on the lower pair. Seam the appropriate sections together with a fine thread. It is a good plan to mark each wing piece so that there is no confusion when assembling them. Cover the upper body with fine black fabric and work double rows of white stem stitch with gold sequins in between. A line of yellow fly stitch comes down the head.

The underbody is in two sections. Cover each with black material and seam them together on the wrong side down the middle, then work branches of yellow fly stitch. Sew the upper and lower bodies together with fine black thread and stuff firmly. Make the legs and feelers by binding fine wire with yellow thread. Have each piece of wire long enough to go up one leg, under the body and down the opposite leg. Turn up the ends of wire before binding. Bend each section round the body and oversew into position in the centre and at each side. Then bend the legs down. Sew the wings on top of the body and have two bright green sequins with gold beads for the eyes.

LADYBIRD

The ladybird (page 101) is made from felt and is slightly larger than the fly. No

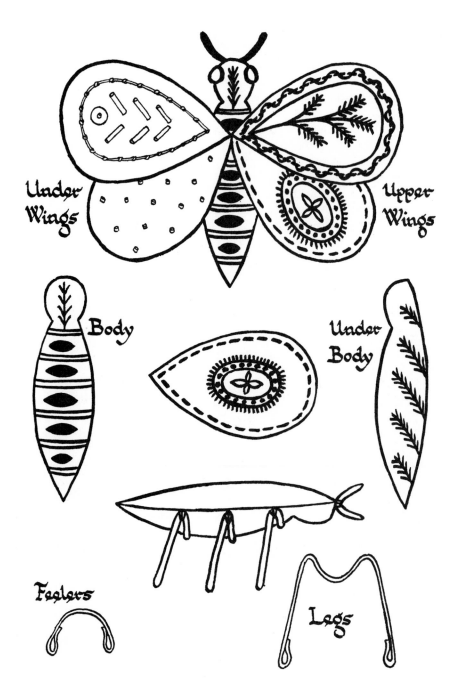

Under Wings

Upper Wings

Body

Under Body

Feelers

Legs

Pattern for Wasp

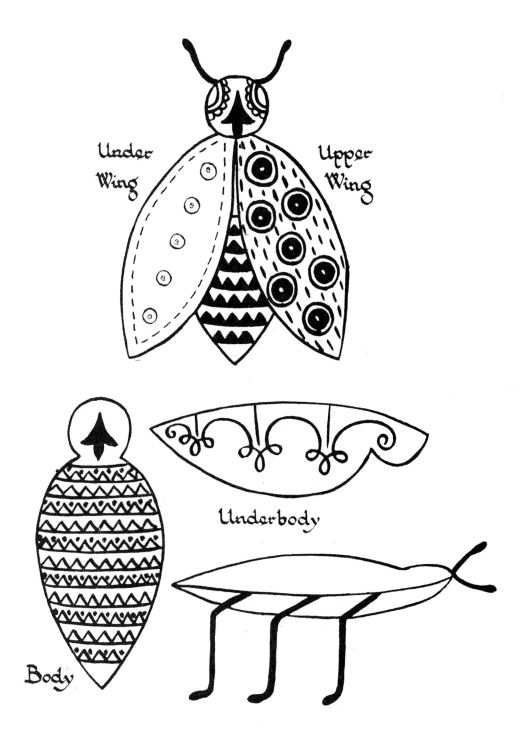

Under Wing

Upper Wing

Underbody

Body

Pattern for Ladybird

paper shapes are necessary.   Cut two upper wings from black felt.   Embroider these with fairly close rows of white running stitches.   Then add bright green sequins stitched on with white beads and encircled with scarlet chain stitch.   Cut two under wings from purple felt.   Work a white running stitch a little way from the edge and sew silver sequins up the middle.   Seam both sections of wings together with matching thread.

The upper body is red felt decorated with rows of green vandyke buttonhole and white beads fitting into the spaces.   Cut the pieces for the under body from white felt. Seam them together down the middle.   Embroider the loop design in black coral knot and stitch on three large green sequins along the middle.   Make the legs from wire covered with black thread.   Assemble the body sections, fixing the legs in between the seams as you go along, and giving them an extra stitch so that they are secure.   Stuff the body firmly.   Be careful with the legs, which will pass right through the body.   Make the feelers as you did the legs, binding with white thread.   Sew them to the front of the head. The eyes are bright blue sequins within a circle of small bronze beads.   Lastly sew the wings into position.   You will see that this insect has warm, gay colours on the upper surface with cool duller ones underneath.

FISHES

Fish shapes are on the whole fairly simple, especially the larger ones.   You can of course make them quite elaborate, particularly some of those beautiful exotic tropical fish with fan tails, glowing colours and more complicated shapes.   The simpler outlines, however, allow one to make greater use of stitchery and design within the shape.

I have included one or two patterns for fish, but hope that you will go on creating them for yourself.   The large fish (page 103) is made from two side pieces with an under-gusset pointed at each end and stretching from tail to nose.   Most of the embroidery is in thick soft cotton.

Cut one side in bright pink felt and the other in turquoise.   On both sides work couching in a double white thread along the scallops, winding the end round to form the eye.   The branches between the scallops are chartreuse green fly stitch.   The curved lines along the middle are black buttonhole with the spokes pointing to the tail end.   The lower of the two lines along the centre is worked with black rosette chain and the space above filled with herringbone—pink on the blue side, and blue on the pink.   The space between this and the top scallops is filled with white French knots worked in three strands of stranded cotton.   Grey coral knot triangles along the bottom are filled with fine blue or pink detached chain with green fly stitch between them.   Blue or pink rows of running stitch are on the tail.   Cut the crest and gusset from bright blue felt and decorate the gusset with fairly large white running stitches.   Sew the fish together with fine cotton, stitching in the crest as you go along.   Then cover all the seams and the scalloped edge of the crest with a couched thick white thread.   Finally couch three rows of black thread for the mouth.   Although I have given all the stitches and colours for the fish, you would have much more enjoyment if you devised stitch patterns for yourself and chose your own colours.

The two small fish (page 105) have no gusset at all.   They are made from silk and taffeta and might look attractive on the Christmas tree.   The first has little embroidery,

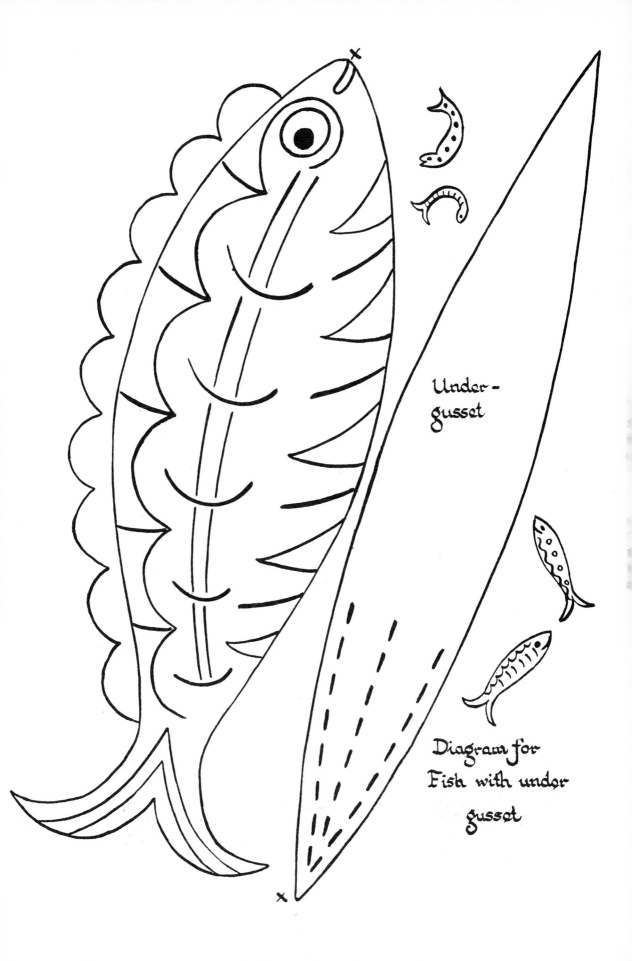

Under-
gusset

Diagram for
Fish with under
gusset

depending more on the fabric for its decoration. Each section is cut in paper first and then each side cut in half along the central line. The top halves are covered with lemon taffeta and embroidered with chain stitch bands of grey, black and grey. The lower halves are covered with black taffeta with tiny painted gold stars on it. You could of course embroider spots of yellow on plain black. The fins are of finely striped grey and white taffeta. Remember to cover two pieces for each fin. On the tail work two rows of black chain. Sew the fin sections together along the outer edges. Sew the top and bottom body sections along on the wrong side. Then seam the two sides, inserting the fins in position as you come to them. Stuff gently but firmly. Make the mouth with two rows of scarlet chain stitch.

The second small fish depends solely on embroidery for the decoration. Cut the two sides from white taffeta and the fins from lemon taffeta. The top and bottom fins may be all in one piece. Embroider the body in bands of jade rosette chain, two rows of black coral knot with black and lemon threaded backstitch in between, and red chevron. The eye is black buttonhole, black coral knot and jade satin stitch. There are jade running stitches under the chin. Rows of black running stitch divide up the fins and there is black double chain on the tail. Once again remember to make two sides for each fin. Sew them together with fine cotton. Stitch up the two sides of the fish, placing the fins in position and stitching through them as you go along. Stuff the fish and work two rows of scarlet chain for the mouth. Finally lay a thick black thread round the fins and tail only and couch down along the edge.

SEA-SERPENT

For the curved sea-serpent (page 106) you will need a curved pattern. Do not attempt to cut a straight strip and twist it round. You will find that the curved shape cuts into quite a large piece of felt, and the finished creature will appear a little narrower than the diagram because of the stuffing. The one illustrated was made in felt but I can visualize a gorgeous glittering serpent of brocade or satin with all manner of iridescent spangles and beads gleaming along its back.

Cut out the top side from lime-green felt and the underside exactly the same from navy-blue. Embroider the design in two strands of cotton. The diamonds are royal blue buttonhole on the outside, then navy running stitch and scarlet chain with a large navy detached chain in the centre. The loops are dark red chain with white detached chain in the middle. For the eyes work circles of close royal blue buttonhole with a circle of white buttonhole on the outside. A navy line of coral knot comes up from the nose with branches of red fly stitch on each side. On the tail there is royal blue threaded backstitch. On the underside make a row of lime green running stitches right round the edge and a line of separate fly stitches in the same colour down the middle.

Before stitching it together make the fins, and mark their positions on the body. The upper sides are of dark red felt embroidered with even rows of white threaded backstitch. The under sides are white covered with dark grey French knots. Seam the fin pieces together with fine white thread. Then sew up the body, fixing in the fins and stitching through them as you go round. Stuff gently with small pieces, taking care not to stretch the felt out of shape.

Fish with two sides and inserted fins and tails

Sea ~ serpent

Section Six

MORE COMPLEX CREATURES

THIS SECTION IS A KIND OF REVISION and has patterns of rather difficult animals. They are all based on the shapes and methods of the previous sections. Perhaps they will stimulate you to make designs for yourself and experiment with different fabrics or make additions to the patterns shown in the diagrams.

ROCKING BIRD

The rocking bird (page 108) is entirely worked in felt and restricted to three colours —red, black and white. Most of the decoration is in the form of appliqué.

First cut the two sides of the bird—one black and one red. For both sides cut the scalloped neck band and the spots from white felt. Cut cleanly with sharp crisp edges. The spots are better if cut out with a leather punch. Hem all these pieces in position, using a fine needle and thread.

Cut out a black and a red wing. The circular motif is white in each case with varying sized holes punched in it. Hem it on to the wing and work three lines of white stem stitch. Then sew this wing shape on to the side of the bird, black on red and red on black. Work a few white detached chain stitches along the lower body. Make the gusset of white felt with alternate leaf shapes of red and black. The tail piece is all white with red appliqué on one side and black on the other. Stitch them together with a piece of card in between. There is a black circle of felt with black buttonhole for the eye on the red side and the same in red on the black side. Sew up the bird and stuff, stitching in the tail last. Make a stuffed white felt beak and sew it in position.

The bird is on a solid rocker. Cut pieces of black and red felt to the half-moon shape in the diagram. Then, also in black and red, cut the scalloped decoration, clipping out the holes cleanly. Hem these pieces on their opposite colours, not forgetting to sew round the insides of the holes. Then cut two more half-moon shapes of felt and two pieces of firm card slightly smaller. Seam the two felts together—a patterned and plain piece with the card in between. For the top cut an oblong of white felt to the size in the diagram, and decorate with a red leaf shape on one end and a black on the other. Cut a second piece of felt the same size and card to go in between, and seam these together.

The underneath of the rocker is made in the same way—of white felt with a red and black shape at each end. It should be long enough to stretch round the curved edge of the side piece. When all these sections are ready sew them together so that they make a solid shape. Be careful with the bottom piece—bend it gently round the curved edge. Sew the bird into position on the top. You will need a long needle for this so that you can push it through from side to side. Finally couch a double row of thick black cotton round all the seams of the rocker. For the couching stitch use white stranded cotton.

Tail

Rocker

Undergusset

Pattern
for a rocking
bird

TORTOISE

Now (page 110) we have a little flat crawling animal rather like the lizard described earlier. The tortoise is made from finer fabric, however, so each piece should be tacked over paper.

Cut two side body shapes and cover with bronze silk. Remember to have them facing opposite ways and you will not get two for the same side. Work white French knots on the neck and head, two rows of white chain across the legs and black vandyke buttonhole for the feet. The underbody is all in one piece, fine lemon spun fabric. Embroider this with jade green fly stitch down the middle and on the tail end. Two branches of red fly towards the head and the spots of red chain. Three lines of black chain are under the chin, two curls of black buttonhole on the front legs and two branches of black fly on the back legs. Seam both sections of the upper body together along the back, then sew to the underbody. Stuff carefully, using very tiny pieces on the end of a knitting needle or something as slender. Lay a thick white thread round all the seams and couch down with a fine red cotton. The eyes are dark green sequins surrounded by small purplish green beads.

Now make the shell. The pattern is similar to the top of the body. Cover both sections with black cotton fabric and embroider a jade vandyke buttonhole round the edge after seaming the sections together down the back. Cover all the space left with even rows of small gold sequins. Those on the original were saucer-shaped, turned upside down and sewn on with tiny gold beads which made little knobs on top. Then cut a strip of red felt with the pinking shears and sew underneath the shell so that only the points appear below it—like a red woolly waistcoat. Finally sew the shell over the creature's back, attaching it here and there with invisible stitching. This is a lovable little tortoise but is rather fiddling to handle, as the shapes are so small. Children, unless very skilful with their fingers, might find it difficult.

PIG

The pig (page 111) is a solid squarish shape, easy to assemble but with quite a large amount of embroidery. Although the legs are narrow they are so short that wiring is not necessary. You will see that the top edge of the gusset bends outwards instead of inwards as all the other animal gussets do. This gives extra plumpness to the creature and is suitable in the pig.

The outside is made from dark red cotton fabric. Cover the sides and back gusset shapes and seam them neatly together on the outside. The back gusset extends from the tail right round the snout to about $\frac{3}{4}''$ under the chin. The embroidery is contained in a broad band which extends over the back and down the sides. Work it right round in a continuous band.

Starting from the middle we have scarlet straight stitch stars within circles of lime green vandyke buttonhole. The entire space round these is filled with white detached chain stitches. On each side of these there is a line of green chain and a line of white. Immediately next to this a row of bright peacock green single fly stitch, then a line of white herringbone threaded with red. The single fly stitch and two rows of chain are

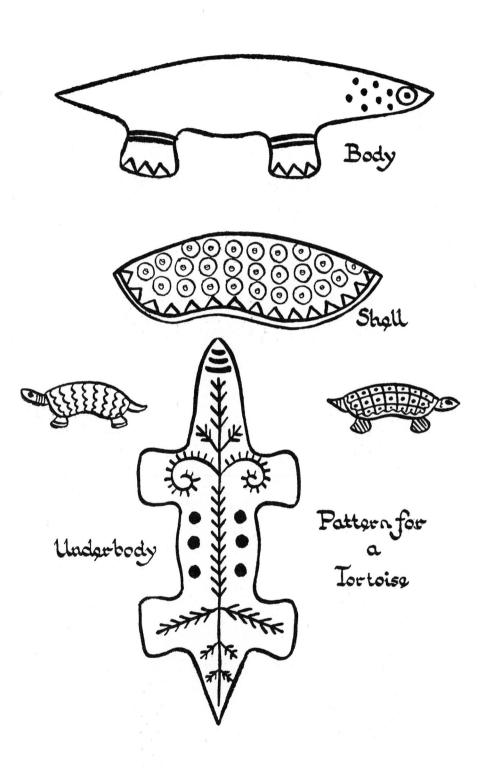

Body

Shell

Underbody

Pattern for
a
Tortoise

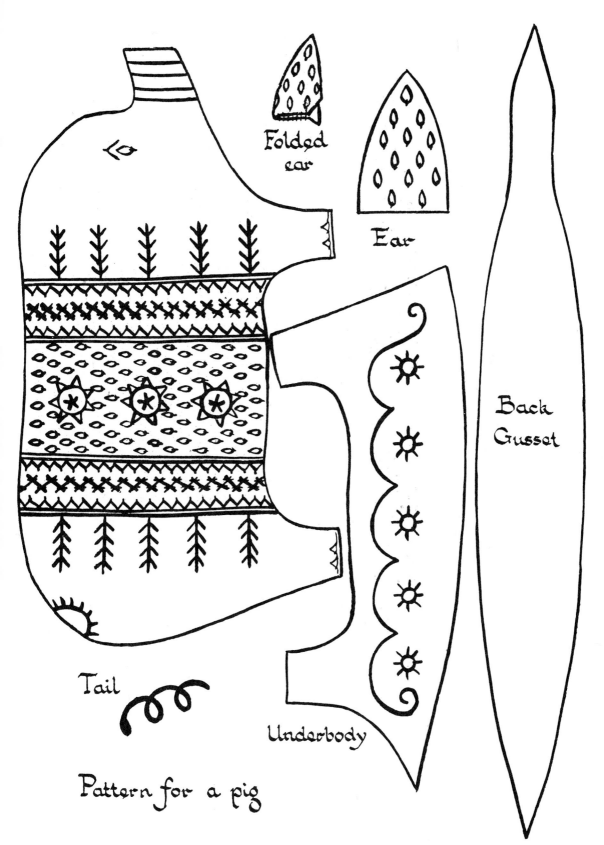

Folded ear

Ear

Back Gusset

Tail

Underbody

Pattern for a pig

repeated on the other side of the herringbone. Scarlet fly stitch branches spring out to the front and back of the band.

Work a line of green feather stitch down the forehead and bands of white coral knot round the snout. The nostrils on the end of the nose are two red detached chain stitches, and the little piggy eye is a green single fly stitch with two red detached chain stitches —one inside the other—underneath it. Work red vandyke buttonhole along the feet. The underbody gusset is rather stiff white corded silk decorated with scallops of green chain and circles of red buttonhole. Seam the two sections along the middle and then stitch them to the body, leaving a space open for stuffing. Stuff gently, especially the narrow legs. Seam up the opening.

Make the ears from red cotton fabric to match the body and work the outside with white detached chain. Fold the ears in half, chain stitching on the outside, and seam the ends together for about three-quarters of the way along. Open out the two little edges left into a V and sew on to the head. The ears will fall forward a little.

Make a tail from wire covered with green silk. Twist it into a curl and insert it at the end of the gusset. Work a circle of white buttonhole round it.

CAMEL

The patchwork camel (page 113) is a little more complex. He is made in four colours. For one side cut the body from navy blue felt, the head from fawn and the legs from orange. Fit these sections together. It is a good plan to try them over the complete side shape to make sure the legs are at the right angles. Secure them with pins and then very carefully stitch them with navy blue fishbone stitch. If you have cut them accurately they will fit perfectly.

Now transfer your design on to the felt. The back leg has the main line worked in navy chain stitch with white running following it on the inside. Jade buttonhole is round the outside of each loop and jade detached chain follows the whirl at the top. The front leg has the zig-zag worked with feather and chain alternately. In the spaces there is a jade straight stitch star with white detached chain between the spokes. Work the circles which run along the back of the body with white vandyke buttonhole and inside each one embroider a knob of jade chain surrounded with a ring of orange chain. Join all these with a line of jade fly stitch. Fawn French knots are on the humps. The scallop along the neck and body is jade coral knot with orange buttonhole worked immediately underneath. Fill the front body with fawn detached chain and embroider the loop design with fawn chain stitch also. Round the head there is jade coral knot. The eye and nostril are white.

The other side of the camel has fawn for the body and jade for the legs, and navy for the head. The design is the same but worked in different colours. Down the back leg orange chain stitch, navy running and white buttonhole. On the front leg white feather and chain, orange stars and navy detached chain. On the fawn body part work navy detached chain and navy continuous chain for the loop pattern, orange coral knot and jade buttonhole for the scallops and orange fly stitch for the line along the back. The circles are white vandyke buttonhole with orange and navy chain inside. Navy French knots are on the humps, orange coral knot round the head, with the eye again white.

Camel

Ear

Sole

The underbody is cut by the dotted line on the diagram, one piece orange and the other green. They are both embroidered with evenly spaced detached chain and fly stitches in navy blue, one line along the body and one down each leg. Seam together all the pieces as for the other animals, leaving a space for stuffing. The legs, being so slender, must be wired. You can stuff from the foot end for a little way and then sew in the navy-blue soles. These each have a stalk of fawn fly stitch. Work the mouth after the stuffing in solid white chain stitch.

Cut the ears from green felt, fold over the sides so that they meet in the middle along the bottom edge, and sew in position. The tail is a narrow tube of orange felt with a tiny white tassel stitched into the end. The fringe, which extends down each side from the chin to the front leg, is made from white rayon cord. Make it as you would a fringed mane. Stitch it very firmly to prevent fraying and then sew on to the camel. Then cut it and fray it out. This is quite easy if you stroke the strands gently with a needle. Make tiny fringes to go round the top of each hump.

DONKEY AND CART

The donkey and cart (page 115) is a fairly simple toy. Make the animal from grey woollen fabric, tacking each section over a paper shape. The embroidery is carried out in two strands of lemon and black thread. Work the centre of the flowers in black chain stitch and the petals in lemon coral knot. In each petal at the centre work a lemon detached chain stitch. Each leg has a line of black chain with lemon detached chain one worked inside another along each side. Eyes, nostrils, and mouth are black. Sew up the animal with matching thread and stuff it carefully.

The mane is fringed yellow raffia. Cut it fairly short after stitching it on. The tail is a bound one made of raffia with a fringed tuft at the end. Make the ears of grey fabric too and work black fly stitch down the inside. For the harness and reins have a very narrow piece of pinked felt or a fine lemon twisted cord.

The cart is made in the same way as the rocker for the rocking bird. The outside is blue felt and the lining red. Cut two blue and two red sides to the shape in the diagram. Then cut a long strip of both blue and red to stretch round the curved edge of the side to make the bottom of the cart. This piece measures $2\frac{1}{2}'' \times 6\frac{1}{2}''$. Embroider all the red pieces with white straight stitch stars evenly spaced. The floral design on the side of the cart has grey chain stitch and fly stitch stalks with lemon detached chain for the leaves. The flowers are red detached chain all worked from a central point. Make a similar design for the long strip and work it in the same colours. Sew a scalloped or pinked edge along the top sides of all the pieces. This looks attractive in lemon felt.

Now cut stout but pliable card slightly smaller than the felt shapes. Sew the matching pieces together with the card in between. Then stitch the long strip to the two side sections. Finally couch a double line of thick red cotton round all the seams, including the top edge.

Both sides of the wheels are made of lemon felt. On the outer side cut a second piece of scarlet felt a little smaller, and pink the edge. Sew it on with dark blue stitching, fitting the stitches into the serrated edge. Then sew on a small circle of yellow felt in the centre. Work dark blue fly stitch spokes springing from this. Sew both sides together

Back-gusset

Donkey and Cart

Ear

Side of cart

Wheel

115

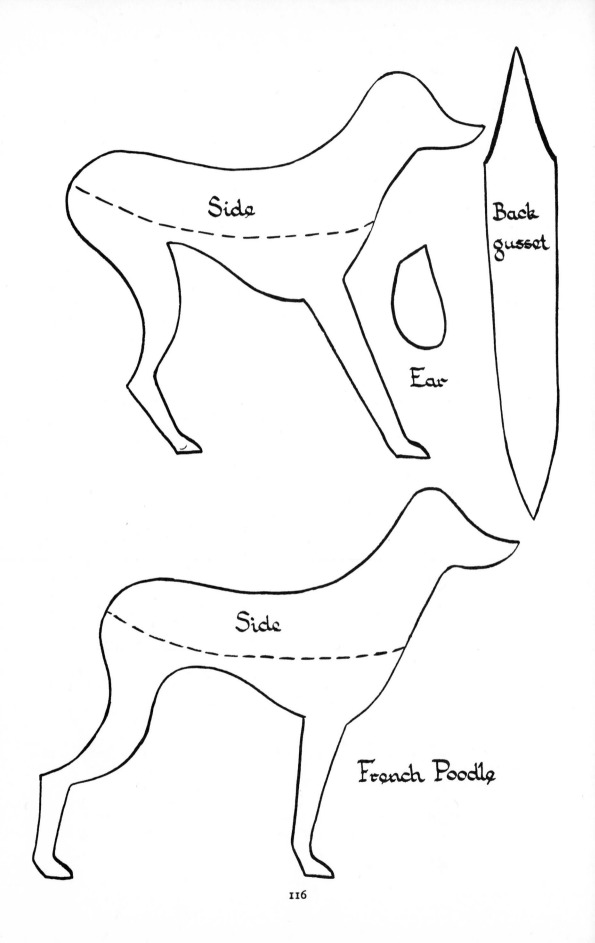

Side

Back gusset

Ear

Side

French Poodle

with a circle of card in between. Then couch a thick blue thread round the outside. Stitch the wheels carefully, invisibly and firmly to the cart.

Each shaft is a double piece of millinery wire enclosed in a strip of red felt. Sew the edges of the felt with fine matching thread and then twist a thick blue cotton along the entire length, securing it at each end and pushing the loose ends inside the felt. Sew the shafts in position to the cart and the sides of the donkey.

Instead of a cart the donkey would look attractive with two baskets, one on each side. These could be made of felt alone if it were fairly substantial, or card covered with felt. They could be attractively embroidered too and would provide containers for gifts or sweets. Or you might like to make raffia baskets. Take a few fine strands of raffia and wind the end into a small coil. Then, with a needle threaded with a strand of raffia, stitch it into position. Continue winding the raffia round, binding and stitching it to the previous row with a threaded needle. You can wrap round once and stitch once, or make more bindings in between the stitches—whatever you prefer. Do keep the whole basket small in stitch and thickness, so that it is in keeping with the size of the donkey. It will not then look clumsy. When your coil is large enough for the base, start to build up the sides gradually, shaping outwards. An extra coil round the top would make a rim. Sew the two baskets together with raffia and bind it as you do for a tail. This piece then rests across the donkey's back.

FRENCH POODLE

The French poodle (page 116) has no embroidery at all. Its trimmings are sufficient in themselves. Cut all the shapes from black or white felt. Notice that the under gusset has two different shapes—one to match each side—as this is a walking animal. Sew up the creature with fine white thread. The legs are very thin, so wire them. Then stuff very carefully, using the tiniest pieces on the end of a knitting needle. Otherwise you will have knobs of stuffing wedged in the legs and you will not be able to move them at all.

Embroider an eye and nose with black thread. Then make a series of fringes from rayon cord. See that they are long enough to stretch round the body. Sew them firmly along the edge and then after slipping them off the card, sew round the poodle. Continue with these until you have the number you wish. Only then cut them and fray out the ends. They can be clipped further into shape with sharp scissors if you wish. Make tiny anklets in the same way.

The tail is a wire covered with white thread and a tuft of the same frayed rayon cord at the end. You might even add a bow to the top of the poodle's head—or one on its tail. The ears are of single white felt stitched in position with white thread.

ELEPHANT

This elephant (pages 118–19) made in white felt is quite elaborately decorated, but he would look just as well with simpler embroidery, or in another colour scheme.

Cut out all the shapes, except the tusks and ear linings, from white felt, and work the embroidery before assembling them. The round motifs on the body have in the centre a cerise sequin, then four small gold beads alternating with four navy detached chain stitches. A circle of jade green chain, surrounded by a second one of cerise single fly

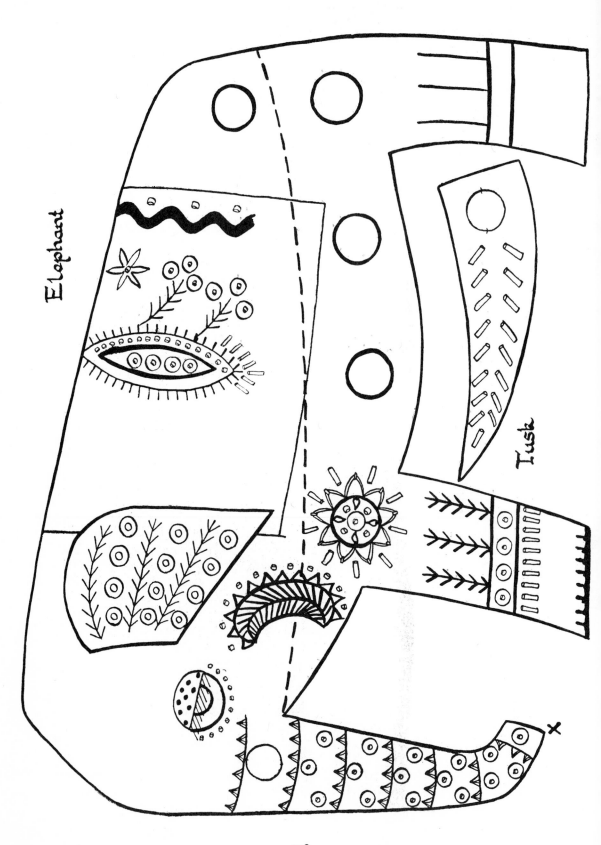

Elephant

Tusk

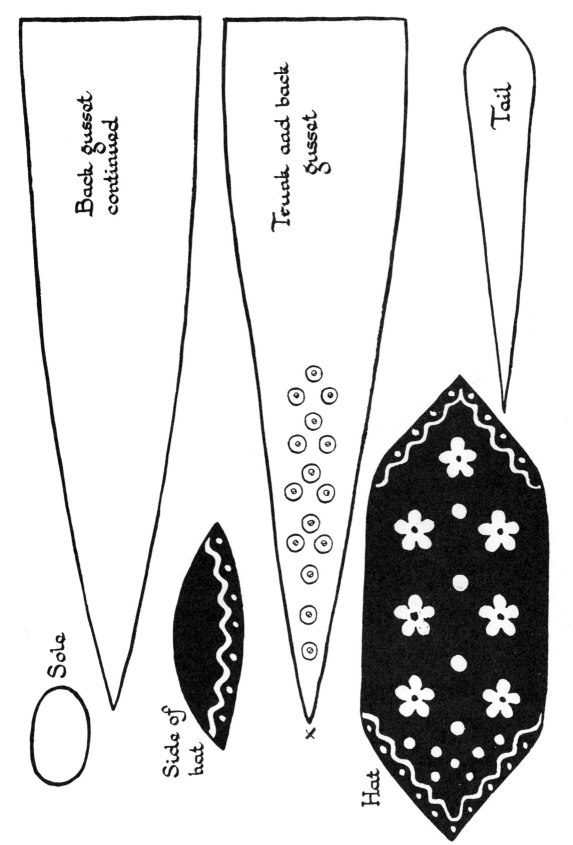

Back gusset continued

Trunk and back gusset

Tail

Sole

Side of hat

x

Hat

119

with long white glass beads coming from the spaces, completes the motif.   The legs have three stalks of jade fly stitch, two rows of navy chain with bright green sequins sewn on with cerise beads between them, and a row of long gold beads underneath.

Down the trunk work rows of navy vandyke buttonhole and in between stitch groups of sequins, three cerise, three green alternately with a large cerise one at the top.   Gold beads are used for attaching these.   The eye is navy chain for the upper lid filled with French knots and fringed with long sloping buttonhole.   The pupil is filled with navy chain with the bottom line in the same stitch.   Then sew a row of cerise beads underneath.

The gusset is shown in two pieces in the diagram, but join them together when making your pattern, and cut it in one long strip.   It extends from the end of the trunk to the tail.   On the trunk end sew groups of green sequins in threes to correspond with those on the side of the trunk.   The half-circle round the site of the tusk is jade chain on the inside line and vandyke buttonhole on the outside, with gold beads in between the stitches.   The centre space is filled with cerise fly stitch.   On the soles of the feet work a violet fly stitch.   Sew all the parts together with fine white fishbone and stuff firmly.

The underbody is shown by the broken line on the diagram.   Round the join of the leg and sole work a navy buttonhole stitch.   Make the ears from a piece of white felt for the outside and violet for the inside.   The white part has branches of navy fly stitch with silver circles or sequins sewn in between.   The lining has biggish white glass beads scattered on it.   Seam the two sections together and sew in position.

The tusks are of violet-coloured felt.   On the outer section sew a large green sequin at the top and then two sloping rows of long white glass beads.   Seam the sections together and stuff firmly.   Sew carefully into position just in front of the half-moon shape on the body.   The tail is white felt seamed together nearly to the top.   The rounded end is sewn on to the elephant.

Now the animal is made you can fit a piece of paper over the back and cut a saddle cloth.   That in the diagram is of violet felt corresponding with the tusks.   It is very elaborately worked with a loop design on the back in jade green chain stitch surrounded by white beads.   On each side there is a leaf shape in cerise buttonhole and within this a row of white beads, white chain and green sequins.   Gold fly stitch branches spring from it with three cerise sequins on the end.   Long glass beads decorate the end of the leaf.   The whole saddle cloth has bronze ric-rac braid sewn along the edge with little white beads fitting into it.

The cap is also of violet felt.   Cut the pieces from the diagram and try them on the head in paper first.   The side pieces fit along the straight edge of the main section.   The centre is decorated with large flower-shaped sequins, diamanté studs down the middle with silver sequins at the front.   Round the outer edge is the bronze ric-rac with small pearls in between.   Dangling down the trunk is a string of four graded pearls.   Sew the saddle cloth and cap on to the animal.

You need not stop here.   You could make a howdah for its back.   Cut the shapes in paper first—two end sections and four roof pieces going to a point.   Then cut them in card and cover both sides with embroidered felt or satin.   Embroider the inside of the roof and end pieces as well.   Stitch them all together.   Make a base to fit the elephant's back and sew the little house on to it.   For the two open sides you could have curtains

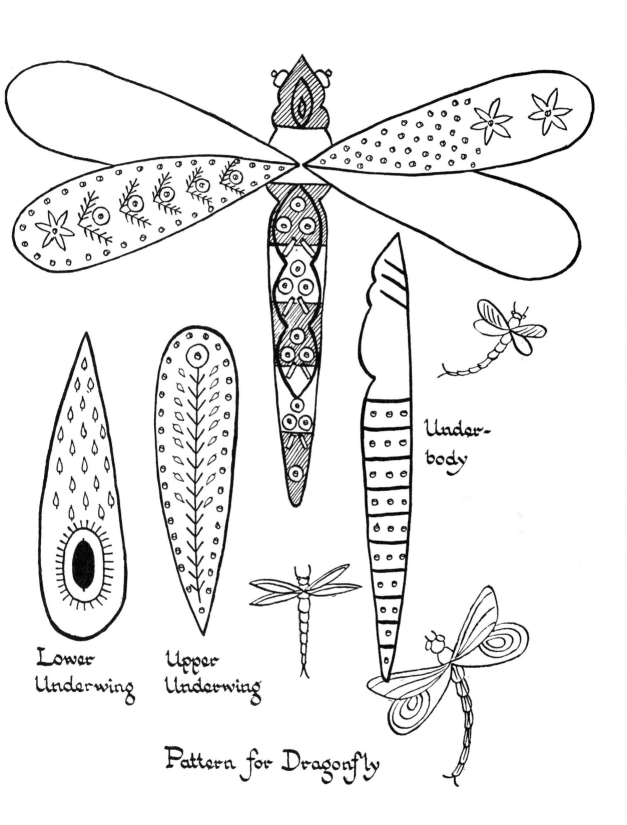

Lower
Underwing

Upper
Underwing

Under-
body

Pattern for Dragonfly

121

made from strings of beads. A howdah with a cone-shaped roof and a curved back piece, with covered wire struts supporting the front of the roof, would look attractive. You could still have the bead curtains round the open section. Alternatively a raffia basket for the elephant's back would look well—filled with tiny felt or pipe-cleaner children.

DRAGONFLY

The dragonfly (page 121) is made in the same way as the fly described earlier. The upper body is of broadly striped grey and white glazed cotton. It has scallops of bright green chain stitch down the sides. In the scallops are alternating groups of royal blue and emerald green sequins, sewn on with tiny beads. Below each group are two long red glass beads. On the head is a leaf of coral knot with a detached chain inside, all worked in green thread. The underbody is plum-coloured felt cut in two sections and sewn down the middle. It has green stripes of chain stitch with rows of gold glass beads in between. Under the head is a wide green fly stitch. Sew up the body and stuff it.

The top pair of wings are covered with white taffeta on the upper sides. Each has a spattering of small pink glass beads with two pearly star-shaped sequins on the ends. The under sides of these wings are covered with a slatey blue taffeta. They each have a line of white fly stitch down the middle with pink detached chain coming from between the arms. Round the edge are pink beads and a silver sequin on the end.

The lower wings also have white taffeta on the upper sides. There are silver sequins down the middle sewn on with blue beads and with branches of fine pink fly stitch. Blue beads are sewn round the edge and a silver star on the end. The under sides are again covered with the blue fabric. White detached chain stitches cover the inner end of the wing, while on the outside there is an oval of pink buttonhole and inside that a large oval-shaped dark blue sequin. Put a very thin layer of card between the wings and seam them together with a fine thread.

Make the legs and feelers of wire and cover with silver thread. Place the legs in position under the body and sew at even intervals with bands of pink thread. Then bend them down. You may have to splay them out at slightly different angles so that they all reach the ground. Sometimes it is a good plan to make the front legs shortest and grade the other pairs in size.

The eyes consist of a large flat white bead with a green sequin on top sewn on with a small silver bead.

Next sew the wings in position. Cover the stitching with a group of green sequins fastened on with silver beads.

ALLIGATOR

The last animal in this section is a patchwork alligator (page 123). Do not attempt this unless you are skilful with the needle.

The animal has three sections to the back. You will see on the diagram that the back is divided by a dotted line. When you are cutting your paper shapes, cut this in two separate sections. The third piece, which is the curved strip in the diagram, fits down the middle of the other two. Cover the two side pieces with white silk, poplin or taffeta and embroider. The zig-zag line is black buttonhole with a gold sequin in each

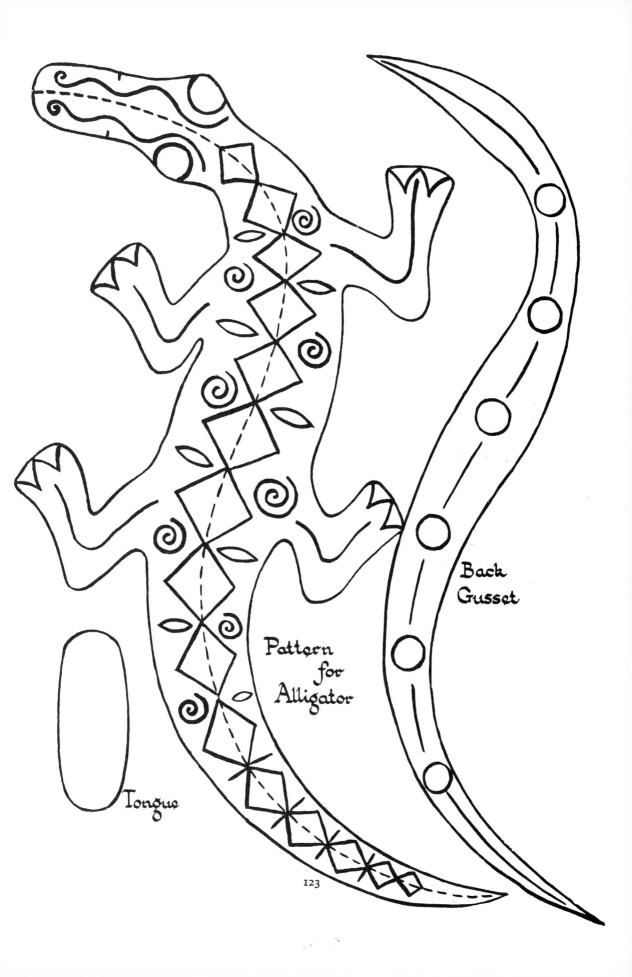

Back
Gusset

Pattern
for
Alligator

Tongue

123

triangular space.   The leaf shapes are filled with red fly stitch and the whirls are green chain with tiny gold beads following round.   Down the legs work green fly stitch with small gold beads on each side and red chain stitch for the claws.   The wavy line on the head is green chain with gold beads filling the inner spaces.   For the eye sew on a green sequin and encircle it with biggish red glass beads.   Cover the middle strip with bright green fabric, something rich to correspond with the elaborate decoration.   The circles are large black sequins with gold beads round them.   The line is red fly stitch with white detached chain fitting between the arms.

Very carefully sew the two side pieces to the central green section on the wrong side, starting at the nose end.   Make your seaming fine and close so that there will be no frayed ends showing, as no doubt you will need to clip the fabric on the curved edges.

The underbody pattern is made exactly to the diagram—all in one piece without the central strip.   Cover it with lemon taffeta.   You may like to work out your own design for it.   It is a good plan sometimes to have a sharp contrast in colour.   The original alligator is embroidered in grey and black only on the underside.   A black chain stitch line extends right down the middle from head to tail.   Black beads are scattered on the back legs and grey fly stitch lines are down the middle of the front ones.   On the body section there are large black sequins alternating with grey close fly stitch leaf shapes attached to the central stalk.   The head part has grey fly stitch branches and black sequins, the tail end grey coral knot scallops along each side of the black line, with long glass beads inside them.

Cover the mouth piece with green fabric and stitch in position.   Fold it in half and sew one half to the upper jaw and the other to the lower jaw of the alligator.   Then finish sewing round the creature—fine and close, especially at corners where the fabric is likely to fray.   The upper body will be slightly rounded because of its extra central section. Stuff very carefully with small pieces.   Cut a long V-shaped piece of red felt and stitch to the back of the mouth for a tongue.   Round the seam of the mouth work a red buttonhole stitch.

TRY SOME EXPERIMENTS

Although I have not given any more patterns for elaborate toys you can continue creating for yourself.   Why not try a rocking horse?   A simple horse shape with the legs sloping forwards and backwards a little, mounted on rockers—stiff card or wood covered with fabric.   Do not forget to add cross-pieces to the rockers to prevent them from splaying out.   A decorative animal or gorgeous bird mounted in an embroidered pavilion would be charming.   Square or round, make the roof and base of covered card and join them together with covered wires.   Decorate the roof, base and sides of the pavilion to make a fitting stand for your creature.   A number of exotic fish hanging from a covered and embroidered circle would be delightful.   Have them hanging at different lengths on fine threads so that they move easily.   If they are decorated with beads and sequins they will shimmer and glitter with the movement.   These are only suggestions which I hope will stimulate you to experiment with ideas of your own.

Section Seven

PAPIER MÂCHÉ TOYS

OR THOSE WHO WOULD LIKE A CHANGE FROM SEWING I am including a section on papier mâché toys. They are made quite quickly and with paints and varnish look extremely attractive.

THIN ANIMALS

The first method is best for thin delicate creatures or those which can be slimmed down successfully without losing their essential characteristics, such as the giraffe or dachshund. You will need some soft pliable wire—the kind used for wrapping parcels is good, or pipe-cleaners. With one piece twist into shape the head, ears, body and tail. One thickness of wire is sufficient. With a second piece put on the front legs. Starting at the foot bend the wire up to the body, twist round securely and then bring down the other side for the second leg. Fasten the back legs on in the same way.

Next you will need some very narrow strips of torn paper—newspaper or tissue paper but nothing harder or thicker. Make sure that all the edges are torn ones. On no account cut them. The soft torn edge sinks into the previous layer more easily and joins are less noticeable.

Paste your long bandages of paper. Flour paste or cold-water paste from the paper-hanger's shop will do nicely. Then bind the wire with the strips of paper, each overlapping the previous wrap like a spiral. Keep on bandaging the wire frame until it is all covered, being especially careful at the joints. Take care not to crease or crumple the strips. If the neck needs to be thicker in one place, wind more strips round it, taking care to graduate the shape. You can build up various parts of the body in this way although it is advisable to keep the whole animal rather svelte. Be sure to wind the strips tightly, particularly the first ones, so that the wire does not rattle about inside when the shape is dry. Keep the surface smooth and finish off with a plain paper. Leave the animal to dry and then paint with poster colour. When the paint is quite dry you can give it a coat of thin clear varnish which preserves the surface.

MORE BULKY ANIMALS

Larger and more bulky animals may be made on a rather more complicated wire frame. Use the same kind of wire as for the smaller ones. Make the shape of the creature as you would draw a side view—body only at first. Then twist circles of wire round the body in appropriate sizes and places to give the animal thickness. Sometimes a little Sellotape helps to hold these sections together. With a finer wire join up these circles, so making a kind of wire mesh body.

The body shape is best kept fairly simple. Once this is made you can add legs by

125

Some shapes suitable for papier mâché

126

twisting them on to the body wires. If they need to be thick and substantial, lace the wire together as you did for the body.

You may add elaborate tails as in the case of birds, or you may make one large tail section which can be painted into different sections at the end. Prehistoric creatures and animals of the imagination are good worked out with this method. Perhaps one of the easiest for a beginner is a fish. You do not then have the difficulty of adding legs. Insects too are good as the legs there have very little thickness.

Even when the wire frame is complete it is not sufficiently substantial to take the first layer of paper. So cover it all over with cotton wadding. This easily pulls apart and beds down well. Bind it on with fine cotton until you have your creature looking as if it had a white woolly coat. If you have hollows in the wire frame which should not be there, it is a simple matter to fill them with pieces of cotton wadding. Make as good a shape as possible.

You will now need some paste and some sheets of soft newspaper and tissue paper. Tear the paper into smallish pieces, discarding any with straight edges. After pasting them stick them onto the cotton wadding, each piece overlapping the other. This first layer is always a bit difficult but the second and subsequent ones are much easier. Be careful to cover every bit of the animal. Where the shapes are small, such as feet, claws, beaks, tails, etc., or where there are curves in the body, you will need smaller pieces of paper. On no account must the paper be folded to fit. The creases will show in the finished animal and they will start to unfold as the paste dries, leaving an untidy rough surface. If you feel you must fold the paper it is a signal to use smaller pieces.

Paste on five or six layers of paper, having newspaper and tissue paper alternately, or different coloured papers so that you can see where one layer finishes and another begins. Finish off with a plain layer. Leave the animal to dry. It will be quite hard and ought to be smooth as well. Paint it with poster colours. There is great scope for pattern and design with the brush just as there is with the needle. It is fun to simplify the characteristic patterns on an animal and translate them into designs of your own making. When the paint is dry finish off with a coat of varnish.

PLASTICINE-BASED TOYS

Another method of making solid toys is to model them first in plasticine. Keep the shape as simple and bold as possible without a lot of fussy appendages. Legs, tails, necks, etc., should be fairly substantial. When the model is finished cover with layers of pasted paper as in the previous method. Once again use soft paper and have torn edges. Small pieces for curves or feet, etc. and no wrinkles or pleats. Have alternate layers of plain and printed paper, or printed and picture paper. Finish off with a plain one as it makes a better surface for painting when the creature is dry. Use a very sharp knife or razor blade to cut down the middle of the animal right round the body—from head to tail. Pull the pieces gently apart and take out the plasticine. It comes away quite readily. If some is stuck in the feet, it is just as well to leave it to weight the animal. Then carefully fit the edges of the shell together and paste strips crosswise over it—two or three layers until it is firm. See that the paper strips sink into the background and that there is no obvious ridge.

Some people advise putting a little fireclay round the inside of all the edges before putting them together. It does make them a little more secure. Be sure the shell is well dry before starting to paint. The more layers of paper you put on the stronger the case, but at the same time too many layers tend to destroy the original shape. This method of papier mâché is used for money-boxes. Choose a good solid animal without a lot of intricate detail—much of this can be painted on afterwards—and cut the opening for the money after you have taken out the plasticine. If it is in the back of an animal half will be in one piece and half in the other. Do see that they match when fitted together again. You can strengthen the edges by pasting strips of paper round them. A pig, horse, lamb, cockerel, or a solid compact figure with hands, arms, etc., painted on it are all suitable for money-boxes.

A similar method of making heads or simple animals on sticks is to crumple some tissue paper on the end of a rod. Make an egg shape if it is to be a head and then cover this with a thin layer of plasticine, moulding in any features or necessary shaping. Then cover with two or three layers of pasted paper pieces. When dry it is ready to paint. In this case the plasticine is left inside the shape and there is no cutting open.

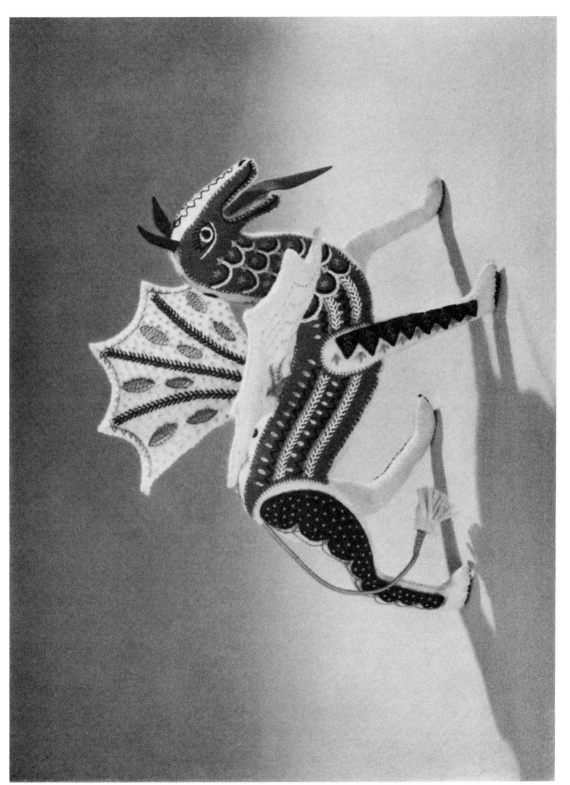

PLATE 5

PLATE 6

Section Eight

CHRISTMAS DECORATIONS

CHRISTMAS IS A WONDERFUL TIME for making decorations. People are often prepared to set to then if at no other season.

You can make and devise delightful decorations for the tree and what is more keep them from year to year, even enlarging the collection each time Christmas comes round. The decorations I have included will last well from one Christmas to another provided they are packed carefully. We all know the joy of opening the box of tree decorations, gently unwrapping them and hanging them in their accustomed places. There is even more fun in making your own glittering toys with your own designs and colours. You will need a collection of beads, sequins, braids, etc., and rich exciting fabrics such as silks, taffetas and brocades. Most of these decorations involve sewing of some kind as a contrast from the paper streamers and toys which last such a short time, and soon become tawdry.

Choose your colours carefully. Too many make the toy look cheap and jazzy. One or two sharply contrasting colours as a general rule make for glitter and sparkle.

GEOMETRICAL SHAPES—DISCS

Some toys are made very simply from geometrical shapes. Start with a circle—drawing round a glass, cup or any circular object of suitable size. Cut your circles from cartridge paper and cover both pieces with fabric. Taffeta, brocade, velvet, woollen fabrics are all suitable. Then sew on your sequins.

The single circle in the diagram on page 130 is in red woollen material with a central motif of a large mother-of-pearl sequin surrounded with royal blue ones. The outer motifs have a silver sequin in the centre with blue ones on the outside. Cut a piece of card slightly smaller in size, place between the two decorated circles and seam them neatly together round the edges. Finish the edge with silver beading, couched silver cord or any other suitable braid. The loop is a string of tiny silver beads. You could vary the circle by having each side a different colour and with a different design. Other flat shapes look attractive made in the same way—a diamond, hexagon, pentagon, etc.

Next try making a number of such discs—perhaps in varying sizes—you could draw round coins—a shilling, sixpence, penny, half-crown, etc. Those in the diagram have white taffeta on one side with red or green poplin on the other. Each side is slightly different in decoration, still maintaining however the red, white and green colour scheme. All the discs are edged with silver cord. Tie each one on to a string of red or silver beads—different lengths—and stitch them on to a small circle of millinery wire covered with red stranded cotton.

Christmas decorations made from geometrical shapes

130

STREAMERS

From here it is an easy step to make the long streamers of the kind you can drape round the tree (page 156). Make a series of decorated discs, squares, diamonds or what shape you will, as described for the first toy, and string them at intervals along a beaded thread or glittering cord. If you choose the beaded thread start by threading a number of beads and then stitching on a motif. Slip the needle through the motif from side to side and start threading the second set of beads. The cord may be slipped through the discs also, but if it is too thick clip one of the outside stitches holding the two sides of the disc together, and poke the end of the cord into the opening, stitching it firmly afterwards so that the cord will not pull out.

CUBES

Now make a series of cubes of different sizes, starting with a small one (page 130 again). You will need six sides for each cube. Cover two sides with white, two with lemon and two with blue taffeta or silk. Make certain that the corners are straight. Then decorate each side. The small one has simply a silver star in the middle of each side—all sewn on with red beads. The middle-sized cube has a silver star surrounded by six evenly spaced silver sequins on each side, while the largest cube of the three has exactly the same with the addition of a silver star in each corner. Seam up all the sides of the cubes with fine white thread and oversewing, having the same coloured sides opposite to each other. Leave an opening for stuffing. Stuff firmly, but not tightly enough to make the shapes bulge, and stitch up the opening. Fasten the three cubes together from the corners with strings of small white beads, having a loop of them at the top. Of course the cubes may be used as separate motifs if you like.

TRIANGLES

Four equilateral triangles stitched together make another easy motif. You can vary them in size how you will. Those shown on page 130 are quite small. Cut each side in paper first and cover with lemon taffeta. Each pyramid is decorated in a different way. The first has a large black sequin in the centre of each side with three gold sequins leading to each corner. The next has a gold sequin in the middle with six black ones round it. The last one also has a gold sequin in the middle and three long black sequins leading to each corner. Seam up the triangles, taking care to fit the corners accurately, and stuff gently—just sufficient to keep the shape. Then make strings of gold beads from the apex of each shape—a different length for each one—and fasten to a small circle of millinery wire covered with gold thread.

Now try stitching together a number of tall triangles to make a motif rather like a spinning top (page 130, third row down on the left). You will need sixteen shapes. Cover eight with lemon fabric and eight with blue. As the triangles are quite small use a thin material. If it is bulky you will have difficulty in sewing them together, particularly at the point. The blue shapes have four silver sequins sewn on with red beads, while the yellow ones have four blue sequins attached with gold beads. Stitch the pieces together in two halves of eight each, alternately the blue and yellow. Then put the halves together, leaving an opening for stuffing. Stuff gently right down into the point,

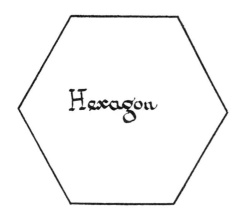

Hexagon

Large Cube

Side for Hexagon Ball

Some shapes for Christmas Decorations

Medium Cube

Side for Spinning top

Side for tall Hexagon

Small Cube

Side for Pentagon Ball

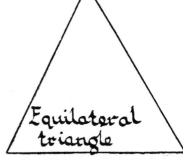

Equilateral triangle

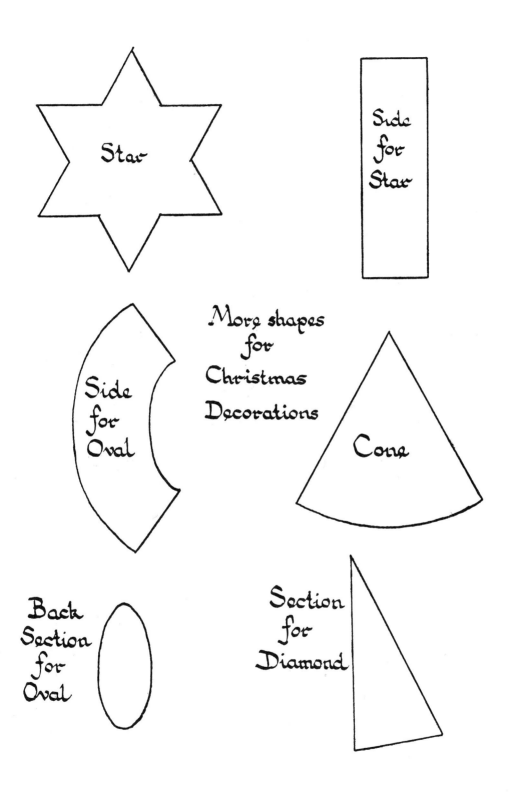

Star

Side for Star

Side for Oval

More shapes for Christmas Decorations

Cone

Back Section for Oval

Section for Diamond

then sew up the opening. Make a loop of gold beads for hanging up, and have two loops of red beads at the bottom, one long and one short, to finish off the decoration.

A charming toy can be made from long and short triangles (page 141). Cut in drawing paper four equilateral triangles and four long ones with the base equal in measurement with the first ones. Cover all the shapes with cerise taffeta. The small triangles have a large silver sequin in the middle and two of them have little white beads round all the edges. The long shapes have a line of white fly stitch down the centre with silver sequins on each side and at the bottom. Again two shapes have white beads all round. Seam all the pieces together, the four small triangles for the top and the four long ones for the bottom. Then join the two sections, having the beaded ones alternating. Stuff the shape gently. Finish off with two loops of white beads at the bottom and one at the top for hanging up.

A STAR

The stuffed star (page 135) is much more difficult to construct but I have included it at this point because it is based on a triangular shape. It needs very careful and neat sewing. You may like to try a larger one first. Cut twenty triangular paper shapes. The star in the diagram has alternate plain pink and narrow grey and white striped sides. Cover the paper with the fabric, making sure that you have all the pieces the right way round. It is a good plan to place them in the star shape as you cover them. They are then easier to assemble without confusion.

Sew the pieces in pairs down the long side of the triangle on the wrong side of the fabric. Then sew these pairs together along the short sides, tucking in all the surplus material. Do this to both sides of the star. Then sew them together on the outside, leaving a space open for stuffing. Be particularly careful at the points. Stuff very gently and seam up the opening. Decorate the centre of the star with a pearly star sequin surrounded with alternate silver and pink sequins. Sew two pink sequins on each point to finish off and have a string of pink glass beads for the hanging loop.

DECORATIONS BASED ON THE HEXAGON

Attractive decorations can be made with a hexagon (six-sided shape) as a starting point. The tall lantern-like toy (page 130, top row) has a hexagon top and bottom with long rectangular shapes joining them. Cut two hexagons and six rectangles from paper. Cover one hexagon and three rectangles with white taffeta and the remainder with cerise. The top white hexagon has a large turquoise jewel in the middle surrounded by gold beads and then turquoise sequins. The base has large pearly sequins alternating with small turquoise ones round the edges.

Sew the side sections together in pairs—a white and cerise—and then decorate them. The one in the diagram has a large gold leaf at the base of each piece with turquoise sequins starting from the centre between the leaves and splaying out to a large pearly sequin on the cerise and a large red one on the white. These are joined up with a curved line of turquoise sequins. The inside of this shape is filled with small gold beads. Join all the side pieces together and stitch on to the base. Fit on the top and sew up three-quarters of the way round. Stuff carefully and stitch up. Make a loop of gold

Circle and star
decorations

beads and have several loops of gold cord hanging from the middle of the base.

The other decoration based on the hexagon is rounder—more like a ball (page 130, bottom left). It is in green and white. Cut two hexagons and twelve side shapes (see page 132) and cover half with white and half with green fabric. The green hexagon has a large silver sequin in the centre with a coil of thick silver cord winding out from it. This can be couched down with fine thread. The ends are pushed through the fabric and fastened off on the wrong side. Do the same for the white hexagon, starting with a green sequin. Each side piece has three sequins at the wide edge in the shape of a clover leaf with four gold beads coming down the middle for the stalk. Use silver sequins on the green and green on the white. Seam all the sections together with fine white thread. It is a good plan to sew them round the hexagon shape first and then seam the sides. Sew both halves together, alternating the colours, and stuff the shape. After it has been stitched up couch a silver cord round the centre seam leaving sufficient at the end to make the loop for hanging.

DECORATIONS BASED ON THE PENTAGON

A pentagon (five-sided) shape works well into a ball (centre of page 130). You will need twelve shapes (page 132), each covered with fabric. See that the corners are sharp so that they will all fit together neatly. Two colours look well on this toy, or a plain fabric contrasted with a patterned one. The ball in the diagram has white material with blue stars printed on it, and the pentagons are cut so that one star fits into the centre of the shape, thus making a basis for the decoration. For six of the shapes it is a deeper blue sequin in the middle of the star, a line of tiny gold beads round the outer edge of the star and then single gold sequins sewn on with red beads in the spaces. The other six pentagons have the gold sequin in the middle with the blue ones on the outside.

Sew up the pieces in groups of six with blue thread, first taking one shape and stitching the other five round it. Then sew up the sides. When both halves are assembled fit them together, the points of one half fitting into the V shapes of the other. Stuff the ball quite firmly so that it will retain its shape. Make a loop at the top of gold beads and a drop at the bottom of several tiny gold beads with two large blue ones on the end.

The star (page 130, top left corner) is more difficult to handle because of the inside corners. When you cover the paper clip into the corners to give a good shape, but do not use a fabric which frays easily. Cover the two stars with white taffeta. The toy in the diagram has a pink pearly star in the centre with silver sequins in groups of three fitting into the star points round it. They are all sewn on with pink glass beads which give a twinkling effect.

You will need twelve rectangular sections which join the two end star shapes together. Cover six with white and six with pink fabric. Each piece has a star at each end with three sequins in between—pink on the white background and silver on the pink. Sew them together in pairs—one of each colour on the wrong side. Then fit the six pairs together so that the pink and white alternate, sewing them on the right side this time. Next fit the stars on both ends, leaving an opening for stuffing. Stuff very carefully right into the points, taking care at the same time not to have the shape bulging. Finally attach a loop of white beads to the middle of one of the long edges.

STAR MADE FROM CONE SHAPES

A cone is a very useful shape. You can use it singly or in groups or, as in the case of the five-pointed star on the bottom right-hand corner of page 130, have it as a beginning of the toy. For this star each cone is hollow and lined with a different colour. Cut ten cone shapes—five a little smaller all the way round. Cover five with white and five with red taffeta or some thin fabric. Sew up the white ones on the right side and the red ones on the wrong. Decorate the white cones with turquoise sequins—perhaps a line of them on both sides. Then place the red linings inside the white outsides and sew round the base.

Next make a small ring of millinery wire and cover it with white stranded cotton—use the full six strands. Then very carefully sew on the cones—attaching them by each side of the base. Make a string of gold beads from the top of one cone for the hanger. Be careful to get the points of this star spaced evenly. If necessary place it over a circle which has been divided into five by measuring 72° on the protractor. If you wished you could fill in the base of the cones with a circle and stuff them. A single one would look attractive hanging with the point downwards, and any number may be used round a circle.

DECORATIONS WITH A RECESS

Another type of decoration is the open one with a recess for a motif of some kind. You can use a variety of shapes, diamond, circle, hexagon, pentagon, etc.

On page 130, at right of second row down, you will find an oval shape. You will need four paper pieces for the outer " frame " and two small oval shapes for the back. Cover the outer sections with red fabric and decorate each piece with two rows of silver sequins, keeping them fairly close to both inner and outer edges. Stitch these sections together in twos along the straight edges on the wrong side, thus making two oval shapes each with a hole in the back. Then place them one inside the other, wrong sides together, and seam neatly round the inner and outer edges. The " frame " is now ready to fit into the small oval back section. Make this by covering the two oval paper shapes with white taffeta and seaming them together round the outside edge. Sew this oval into the hole left in the " frame ". Make a dangling decoration for the middle by having a string of five graduated pearls—largest at the bottom—and two larger loops of biggish red glass beads hanging from the top of the outer rim of the " frame ". The toy in the diagram is finished off with an edge of silver beading, but a couched silver or white thread would look just as well. Finish off with a hanging loop of small silver beads.

A second toy of the same kind (left of second row, page 130) is made from four triangles. This gives only a slight recess, not a deep one, like that of the previous decoration.

Cover eight sections of paper with turquoise silk. See that they are in the correct position before sewing on the fabric. The longest edge of the triangular shape goes to the middle. When you have covered the paper sew the pieces together on the wrong side in fours, one set for the inside and one for the outside. Decorate the inside section with gold sequins round the edge. A bunch of silver-headed stamens is attached just below the middle and a wire threaded with red glass beads twisted into the loops—small at the top and large at the bottom—framing the stamens. The loose ends of the wire are twisted together, poked through the fabric and secured on the wrong side. Catch the small loop at the top on to the background. Now sew the back section to the front round the outer edge. Finish this off with an edging of gold beading and make a hanging loop of small gold beads.

TWO EMBROIDERED CIRCLES

Toys which are a little more substantial may be stiffened with card. A circle is a good starting point. You may have the circle alone or add something exciting to the inside, a bird, star or other geometrical shape, flower, animal or what you will. On page 135 I have shown a flat star within a circle and a rounded bird also in the same shape. These decorations now have a little embroidery added to the beads and sequins, giving an altogether rich effect.

Cut two circle shapes in paper and cover each with yellow silk. The fabric must be clipped on the inside of the ring so that it lies flat. Embroider a line of black feather stitch round the outer edge and then stitch on long bronze beads in a zig-zag line. Cut a card circle slightly thinner in width, place it between the two yellow rings and seam them neatly together round both edges.

Cut two paper star shapes and cover with white silk or taffeta. The star in the diagram has a gold sequin in the middle with long gold beads branching out from it. Leaf-shaped black sequins join these together, and there are three gold sequins on each point of the star. Decorate both stars. Stitch them together with a card shape between. Then fit in the circle and attach the star by each point. Make a hanging loop of gold beads. Of course a more exciting star would be one with each side worked differently—both in colour and design, perhaps delicate on one side and vivid on the other.

The second circle is made from pink silk or poplin. Make it in exactly the same way as the previous one. The embroidery is slightly different. Round the outer edge there is white single fly stitch with bright blue sequins and long white glass beads alternating and fitting into the stitch. The little bird is of white felt, but a lovely satin or brocade creature would look beautiful. Make an undergusset for the bird as for the sitting hen described in the bird section. It is decorated with pink glass beads scattered on the body with a blue sequin encircled with pink beads for the eye. The wings are of single felt with long white glass beads and silver sequins on them. The tail is of double felt with the same decoration. For the crest use feathers or silver-headed stamens. Attach the bird by the head, tail and underbody to the circle and finish off with a loop of pink beads.

FOLDED SHAPES: CIRCLE AND TREE

The next two toys (page 139) are different in that they involve folded shapes. The shapes themselves can be very simple, such as a square or diamond, or a more complex leaf or flower. I have illustrated a circle and a tree. They are both made by the same method.

For the circle cut four paper shapes from stout cartridge paper and cover two with cerise taffeta and two with pale blue. On each blue one embroider the loop design with cerise coral knot. Sew on also two pearly pink stars and a spattering of pink glass beads.

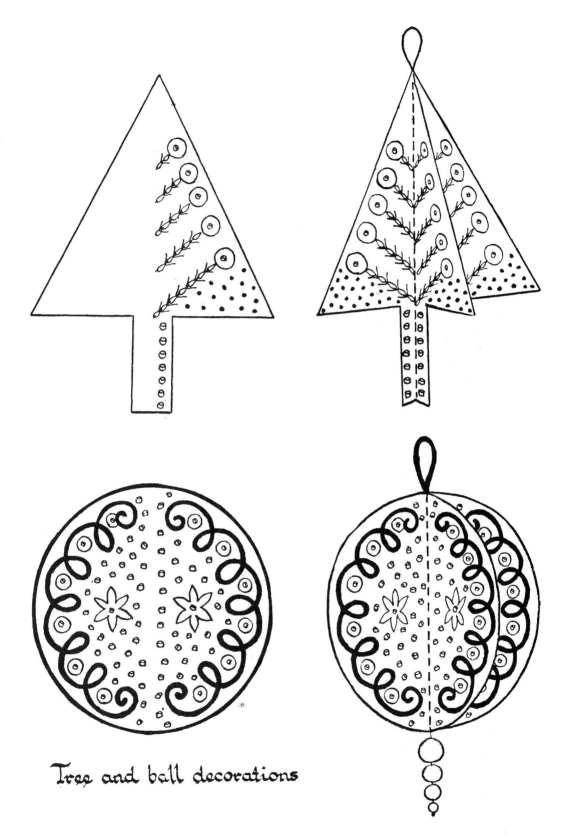

Tree and ball decorations

Repeat the design on the cerise circles in pale blue with silver stars and silver beads. Sew together the two blue circles and then the two cerise ones. Use a fine matching thread and a small seaming stitch. The edges of course may be finished off with beads, braid or cord if you wish.

Place the two covered circles together exactly and sew with a stab stitch right through directly down the middle. Then fold the sections back so that each stands at right angles to its neighbour. Give an additional stitch top and bottom so that they hold this position. Finish off with a loop of silver beads at the top and a drop of four or five medium-sized pearls at the bottom.

The tree is made in green and white fabric. Cut and cover the shapes as for the circle. On the green sections embroider sloping stems of white chain and fly. There are gold sequins on the ends of the branches, black French knots in the corners and gold beads down the stem. The white sections are the same except for the chain and fly branches, which are green. Seam the sections together, then stitch down the centre, fold back and stitch at the top and bottom. Finish off with a loop of gold beads.

COMBINED CIRCLE AND CONES

We now (page 141) have a combination of a flat motif and a rounded one. It is a circle with a cone on either side. The circle can be drawn to any size. That in the diagram is $3\frac{1}{2}''$ in diameter with the cones $2''$ in diameter.

Cover two paper circles with white taffeta and two cone shapes with cerise. Round the edge of one circle are large cerise limpet-shaped sequins and round the other silver stars. Work four evenly spaced branches of white fly stitch on each cone and decorate the ends of the branches with silver sequins. Sew a row of small silver beads a little way from the edge. Stitch up the cones with a matching thread on the right side and stuff them. Place each cone in the middle of a white circle and stitch on firmly, tucking in all the stuffing.

Cut a circle of card slightly smaller than the original ones. Place between the two sections and seam round the outer edges. Make a small loop of silver beads at the top of each cone so that the decorations can be hung from either end. Then make loops of silver beads round the outer edge of the circle. The best way is to fasten your thread to the edge of the circle, then slip a number of beads on to the needle and make a stitch or two a little further round the ring, so that the threaded beads hang in a loop. Repeat this right round.

TOYS MADE WITH WIRE

The next group of toys involves the use of wire. Use the fine sort which easily bends and slips through the smallest beads. It may be cut with an old pair of scissors. Once again I have started with a circle, but of course other shapes will look equally attractive. For the first one on page 141 cover two paper circles with white taffeta. Work each one with five arms of red feather stitch, filling the spaces with black French knots. Place a silver star in the middle and a silver sequin in each space. Cut a card shape for the inside and sew the two taffeta circles round it with crossed oversewing in red. Next take some fine wire and thread on to it some red glass beads, enough to make

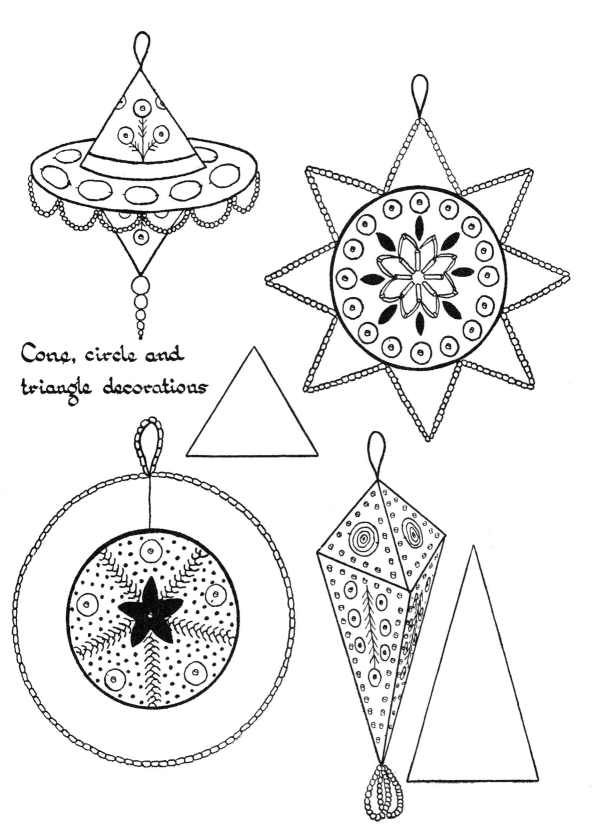

Cone, circle and triangle decorations

a circle about ½″ bigger all round than the fabric one.   When you have reached this size twist the two ends of wire together—once will do.   Do it tightly so that the beads in the ring are firm and close.   Then continue threading a few more beads on each end of wire until you have sufficient to form a loop.   Twist the ends together again—two or three times now—and cut the wire closely.   Hang the fabric circle from the top of the beaded ring by a length of red thread.   Arrange it so that the space left round is even.   The circle will swing about quite freely.

Make the circle for the second decoration in the same way as in the previous one. This time decorate it with long gold beads springing from the centre with black single fly stitch joining them.   Then sew on small black leaf-shaped sequins, fitting them into the stitches with gold sequins in between on the outer edge.   Sew the two circles together with the card in between with crossed oversewing in black.   Take the fine wire and, leaving 2″ or 3″, stitch it firmly to a point on the outer edge of the circle.   Then thread on to the long end a number of gold beads—sufficient to form one point of a star.   Again tie down the wire a little further round the circle.   Continue in this way, threading and tying down at equal intervals until you only have one more point to make.   To make the last point thread beads on both wires—that left at the beginning and that left at the end, until it is the same size as the others.   Twist the wires together once, continue threading on each end until you have sufficient to make a loop.   Twist the wires several times and cut them closely.   It is a good plan to count the beads on each point so that they are all the same size.   Also mark round the circle the places for stitching the wire.   You can nip the points into position after the threading is finished.   The wire may be bent in other ways too, such as scallops, loops or petal shapes.

I would now like to describe one or two toys made from wire, beads and sequins only.   It is fascinating to play about with the wire as it can be twisted into so many designs.   Perhaps those on page 143 will inspire you to try out other ways of your own. The easiest way to begin, I think, is to make a series of bead circles—perhaps three, one inside the other, attached by threads so that they swing about freely.

Then we come to an eight- or six-pointed star.   Take a length of wire a little longer than the distance right across the star.   Thread on one bead and bend the end of the wire up so that it lies alongside the rest of the wire.   Then continue threading beads, pushing them over the double piece of wire until it is covered.   The star in the diagram has six or seven small beads and then a sequin star.   This is repeated twice more and then there is a long string of beads across the middle.   Finish the other end with the stars and beads as at the beginning.   Twist the end of the wire round the last bead and cut it short.

Each other arm of the star is made in the same way, but it must be attached to the first one as you go along.   Start the second arm and thread as for the first one until you reach the middle, then twist the wire tightly round the middle of the first arm between the beads.   Continue threading to the end of the second arm.   You will now have a four-pointed star.   Make two more sections, tying each one round the middle as you come to it.

The star in the diagram has an additional circle round it.   Start this by twisting the wire round one arm a little way from the centre, then thread on sufficient beads to reach

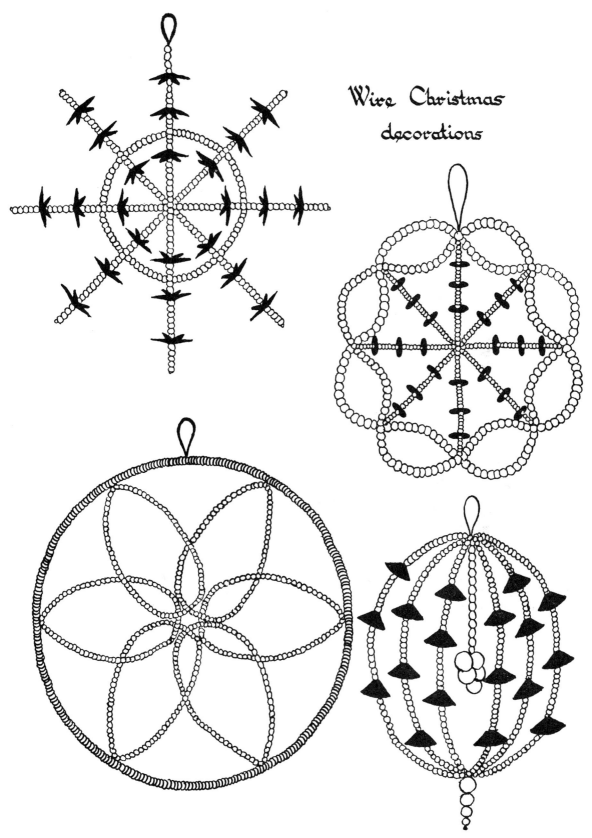

Wire Christmas decorations

the second arm and twist the wire round this.   Continue in this way until you are right round the circle.   Twist the end of the wire tightly round the first arm and cut it short. Finally stitch a silver star on each side of the middle, winding your thread through the wires until it is secure.

The next wire decoration has a similar star within a circle of loops.   Make the circle first by threading on two wires in the following way.   Leave an end of each wire and twist together.   Then thread an even number of beads on to each wire and twist again, thus forming a loop.   Continue round the circle until you have eight loops.   Twist the end of the two wires round the two ends left at the beginning and make them into a loop. This can be covered with thread and used for the hanging loop.

Then make a star similar to the one described previously.   Start by twisting the wire round one of the joints between two loops, and continue by threading on beads and sequins in their order until you reach the joint between the loops directly opposite.   Fasten off the wire here.   Continue joining the loops opposite each other with the arms of the star, not forgetting to twist the wires in the centre each time you cross.   Finally sew a star sequin on each side of the middle.

The petal-shaped wire motif within the circle takes a little more calculation.   First make a circle of millinery wire with a loop at the top.   Mark it evenly into six portions. Twist the fine wire round the outer circle at one of these points and thread on sufficient gold beads to make a petal shape with the rounded end reaching almost to the middle. Fasten the end off at the point where you started.   Make a second petal starting at the next point round the circle.   As soon as you have threaded on enough beads to meet the first petal, twist this second wire round it.   Thread on a few more and twist round the first petal again—thus making a small leaf shape.   Continue threading beads until the second petal is the same size as the first, finishing off at the point where you started.   Make four more petals.   The last one will need to be twisted round the fifth one and the first one to complete the shape.   Finally cover the outer circle and loop with red stranded cotton, using the full thickness.

The last wire decoration consists of four circles of silver beads interspaced with black and cerise limpet-shaped sequins.   These as a rule have holes at each side, but a hole is easily made in the centre with a needle.   Make a circle of beads, interspacing cerise sequins at even intervals.   Remember to have twice as many beads in the space which comes at the bottom of the circle.   Twist the two ends of wire together at the top.   Start a second circle in the same colours.   When you are half-way round twist the wire to the centre bottom of the first ring so that the circles are at right angles to each other. Then continue until you reach the top, fastening the two end wires to the first ones. Make two more circles, using black sequins instead of cerise ones, and fasten them between the first two, making a ball with eight sections in all.   Twist all the ends of wire into a loop at the top and cover with thread.   Sew a drop of pearls at the bottom and another drop of silver beads with a cluster of pearls at the end hanging down the centre from the top.

FRUIT SHAPES—APPLE

Attractive sparkling fruit looks well as a decoration and is made very simply.   Those

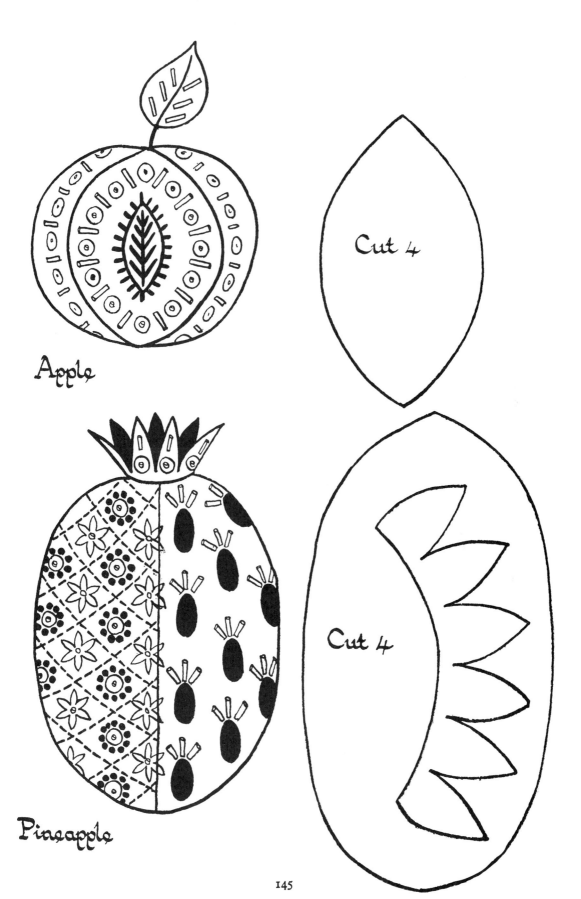

Apple

Cut 4

Pineapple

Cut 4

145

in the diagram are made from felt, but brocade, satin or taffeta could give an even richer and more exotic appearance.

For the apple, cut four shapes, two green and two dark red. Embroider fly stitch and buttonhole in gold thread in the centre. On the red pieces sew on long gold beads and sequins alternately round the edges. Use bronze beads and sequins on the green felt. Seam the sections with fine matching thread and stuff firmly. Make a leaf from one green and one red section with six long bronze beads on each, and a hanging loop of small bronze beads.

PINEAPPLE

The pineapple also has four sections, two red and two white. The red ones are divided into diamond shapes with white running stitch. In each diamond is a silver star or a black sequin encircled with small white beads. The white sections have long, leaf-shaped black sequins with three long red glass beads at the top. All are sewn on with red beads.

Seam the sections together with white thread and stuff carefully. Cut two black felt shapes for the top leaves. Decorate the outer one with silver sequins and long red beads on each point. Sew the two pieces of felt together with matching thread. Then attach in a circle to the top of the pineapple. Make a loop of white beads and fasten to the middle of the top.

NUTS

The nuts have three sections to each fruit—red, blue and lime green. Sew four silver sequins on the blue piece and four blue on the red section. On the green work a row of white single fly stitch along one side and fit long red glass beads into the spaces between the stitches. Sew the sections together and stuff them, but do not finish off until the stalks are made. Cover some lengths of millinery wire with red thread and insert the two ends into two of the nuts. Finish sewing up the nuts, catching in the stalks at the same time. Sew a large red glass bead to the base of each nut. Bend the stalks into two—different lengths—and stitch the bunch together at the bend. Finally make a loop of white beads.

PEAR

Three shapes go to make the pear also, green, pink and black. The design is the same on each section. A line of vandyke buttonhole is worked round the outer edge, pink on black, green on pink and black on green. In the same colours work the central stem and curls in coral knot. The fly stitch branches are green on black, pink on green and black on pink.

The remainder of the decoration consists of beads and sequins. On the black section we have seven green sequins round the top of the stalk, four pink stars on the ends of the fly stitches and pink beads following the curls at the base of the design, also between the vandyke buttonhole round the edge. The green section has pink sequins round the top, pink stars and multicoloured green and purple beads. On the pink piece there are silver sequins, silver stars and the multicoloured beads. Sew the sections together neatly,

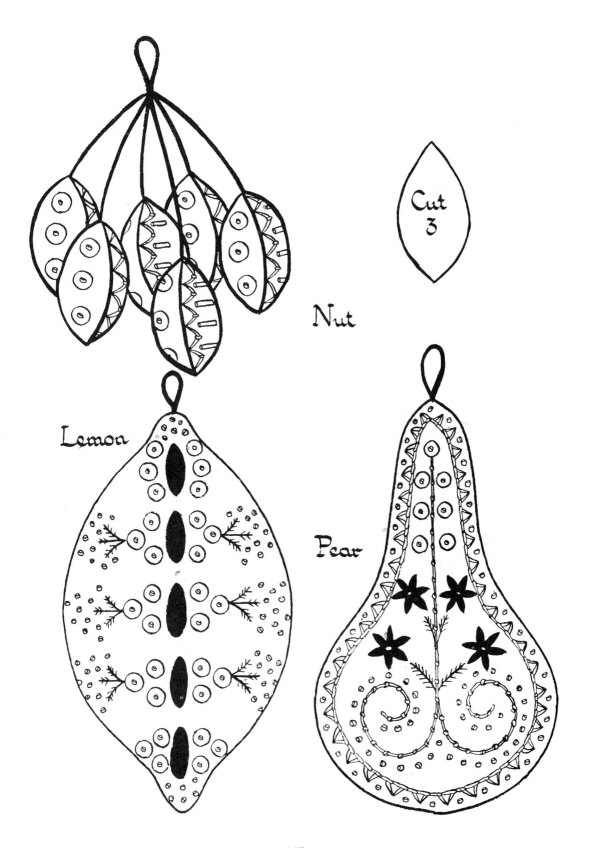

Nut

Cut
3

Lemon

Pear

147

stuff and make a loop of small beads. Cherries, pomegranates, bananas, strawberries or grapes would be good shapes to embroider.

LEMON

The lemon is made in three sections, like the nuts. This time black, white and lime yellow felt is used. The design is the same on each piece, just varying a little in colour. Down the centre of the section is a line of large oval sequins—black on the yellow and white sections and gold on the black. On each side of these oval shapes are groups of three gold sequins. Springing from the top sequins are three small branches of fly stitch worked in one thread of cotton—white on black, red on white and black on yellow. At the top and bottom of each section and also round the outer edges of the fly stitches, small red beads are spattered. Neatly seam the sections together, stuff firmly and make a hanging loop of red beads.

AN ANGEL

No tree is complete without an angel. That on page 149 is small but may easily be enlarged. Its essential quality is delicacy and fragility, so do choose a fabric which expresses these characteristics. The shape is simple—based on a cone. In this case it is hollow so that it may be placed on a branch. Cover two cone shapes with pale blue crêpe-de-Chine. Make one cone slightly smaller than the other. Embroider the outer one with one thread of rose pink. Use the one colour for all the embroidery. The last thing you want is a jazzy effect. The hands are in stem stitch and the sleeves in rows of whipped running. Down the centre front is a little tree of fly stitch with groups of silver sequins and pink stars on the ends of the branches. Round the bottom work scallops of buttonhole stitch with a line of tiny running stitches following the shapes. Sew a silver sequin in each space.

The back has graduated lines of running stitches with sprigs of fly stitch alternating with silver sequins. Seam up the back of each cone and place the plain one inside the embroidered one. Sew them together round the top and bottom.

Make the head. Cut two shapes from the diagram, making the neck a little longer. Cover with the crêpe-de-Chine. Work the hair in rows of whipped running, the downcast eyes in close buttonhole stitch and the mouth with a single fly stitch. Before sewing up the head make a halo of white beads threaded on to a wire. Insert the ends of the wire between the head pieces as you sew them together. Gently stuff the head. Place the neck in the top of the cone and stitch it.

Cover four paper shapes in the same crêpe-de-Chine for the wings—two for each. The back of the wing has a central line of single feather stitch with similar branches towards the outer edges. These have silver sequins on the ends. The inner half of the wing is filled with tiny French knots. The front wings have two rows of scallops in buttonhole stitch with three lines of fly stitch at the top. On the centre line is a pink star with silver sequins on the other two as well as in the spaces between the scallops. A single pink star is sewn in the lower half of the wing. Seam the wing sections together and sew into position on the back of the angel.

Christmas
Angel

149

THE THREE KINGS

A more elaborate but charming decoration based on the cone shape is a set of smaller cones representing the Three Kings (page 151). You could of course change the characters if you wish. Cut and cover three cones for the outside and three more smaller ones for the linings.

The first King is in white taffeta worked with one thread of red, green and black cotton. Work the sleeves with green stem and buttonhole, the hands with red stem and the necklace with black single fly. The branching tree is green fly with a red sequin on each branch. The border comprises a row of red and a row of black vandyke buttonhole followed by a line of red and black threaded running with green detached chain in the spaces. The borders of the cloak are made with black whipped running, with red single chain and fly between. Inside this edge work a row of green buttonhole. Carry the border right round the back of the cone. Fill in the space at the back with red stars.

Arrange your design so that the join comes down the middle of the back. Sew up the cones as for the angel. Make a head from a circle of white silk. Turn in the edge and gather it. Place a hard knob of stuffing in the centre and pull the thread up tightly. Stitch to the top of the cone. Embroider a face on the knob with one thread. You can work hair if you wish. Straight satin stitches from the centre, or side, or wherever you wish the parting to be, or French knots worked very closely, make satisfactory hair. An added attraction would be Kings of different nationalities—a white, a yellow and a black.

Make a tiny crown from a piece of wire threaded with small beads. Twist it into a circle to fit the head and then make a shape over the top from side to side. Sew the crown to the head at each side.

The middle King is made in the same way. He has cerise taffeta worked with lemon and turquoise, with a large silver star in the front. His crown is pink glass beads. Make the third King from yellow taffeta and embroider with red and blue and black. The sequins are blue sewn on with red beads. The crown is of blue glass beads.

Now make the frame to support them. Cut the shape in paper twice and cover it with pale blue fabric. Sew on silver stars at each point and fill the spaces with pink sequins. You can put a piece of card in between if you wish—but have the flexible kind that does not easily crack. Seam the two sides of the frame together and make a hanging loop of blue beads. Stitch the two outside Kings on to the ends by the tops of their crowns and hang the centre one by a thread from the middle, making it as long as you wish so that the three form a complete group. Many other hanging toys of this nature can be made, varying the shape, size, character and number. I have included on page 155 a decoration of three little fish.

TWO TREES

The two trees (pages 152 and 153) are larger than the previous toys. They may be used as individual pieces or even as a basis for a table decoration. They are made of felt but would look very well in some richer fabric.

For the cone-shaped tree cut two shapes in black and two in white felt. Each pair is decorated differently but elaborately with red, black, green, gold and silver beads and

Pattern
for
Cone-shaped
Kings

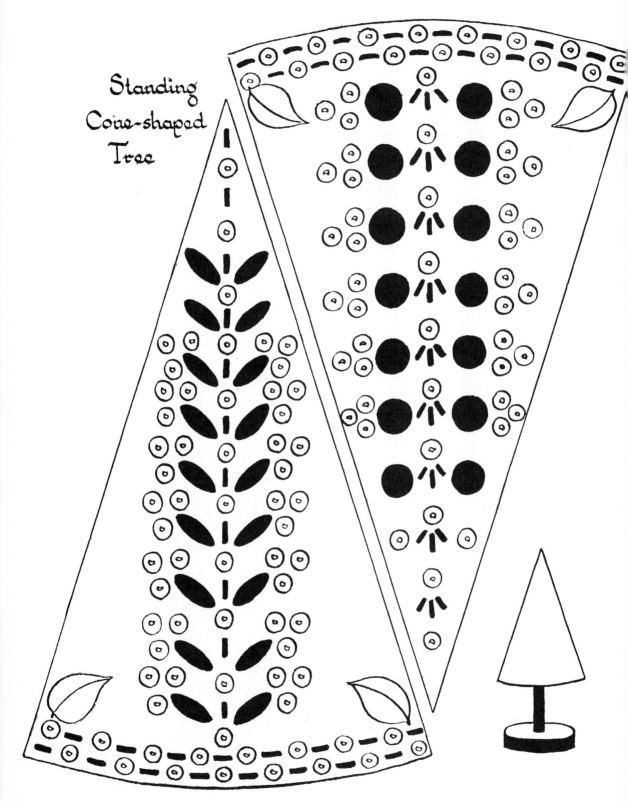

Standing
Cone-shaped
Tree

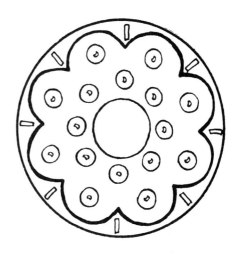

A decorative
tree made from
circles

153

sequins.   There is no embroidery.   You could use the pattern in the diagram or, better still, work out your own.   It is advisable to play about with the sequins before sewing them on until you have a satisfactory design.   When you have completed the pattern sew the sections together with fishbone stitch.

Then cover a 10″ piece of $\frac{1}{2}$″ dowel rod with felt.   You will need a base for the tree. A 4″ circle of wood about $\frac{3}{4}$″ in depth is best—but strong card sections fastened with Sellotape would be quite a good substitute.   That is a top, base and side strip.   Make a hole in the centre of the base to take the dowel rod which forms the trunk of the tree. Cut sections of felt to fit over the base and decorate them to correspond with the tree. Sew these pieces together with the base inside.   Glue the dowel rod firmly into position. It is now ready for the top of the tree.

Cut a circle of felt $5\frac{3}{4}$″ in diameter, decorate the under side and cut a hole in the middle so that it can be slipped over the dowel rod.   Slide this piece of felt down the rod, then slide on a slightly smaller piece of card cut to the same shape.   Leave these two pieces loose at the bottom for the time being.   Now place the cone over the top of the rod and stuff round it firmly.   Then slide up first the card and then the felt circle to meet the base of the cone.   Stitch them together with matching thread, pushing in extra stuffing if necessary as you go round.   You can give a stitch or so in the middle to make the base of the tree more secure.   Finish the seams round the base of the tree and its stand with a couched gold thread.

The second tree has the same base as the first, covered with felt with a central rod for the tree-trunk.   A tapered rod is better for this tree, however, as the stem is visible all the time.   The original is in black and white felt also, with the addition of a little red in the decoration.   Cut three white and three black circles measuring $2\frac{1}{4}$″, $3\frac{1}{4}$″ and $4\frac{1}{4}$″ in diameter.   Cut a hole in the centre of each for the rod.   The black felt is on the under side of each circle and decorated with silver sequins evenly covering the spaces.   All the embroidery on the white felt is worked in black, and silver sequins and long red beads are added.   Now cut three card circles slightly smaller than the felt.   Place in between the felt sections and seam them together both on the inside and outside.   You can finish off the edges with silver beading or cord, or loops of beads.   Cover the rod with black felt.   A red, white or silver cord twisted along its length enhances it.   Slide the largest circle on to the rod first and stitch into position round the centre stem.   Then the middle circle a few inches above and finally the smallest one.   Leave a little of the tapered end showing at the top, and decorate the end with a tassel or loops of cord.   It is a good plan to try the circles on the rod first by pinning so that you have them in the best position before the final stitching.

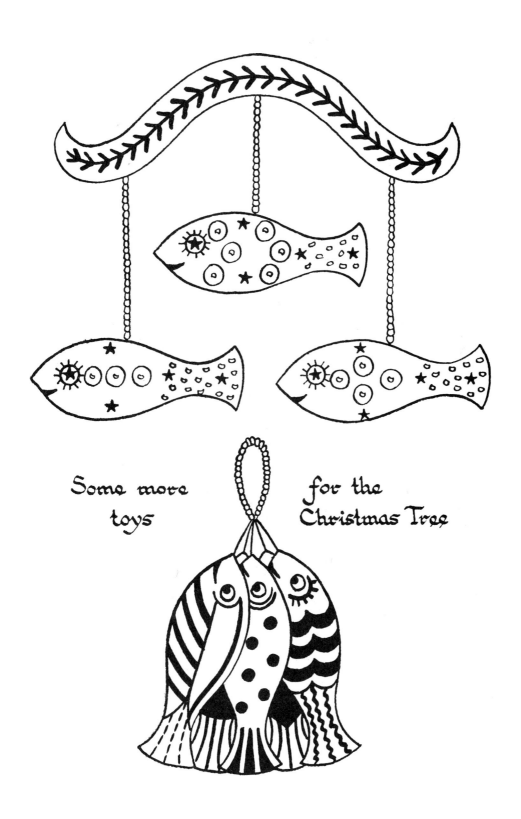

Some more
toys
for the
Christmas Tree

A Christmas streamer

Section Nine

DOLLS AND THEIR CLOTHES

O F ALL TOYS, dolls hold the greatest fascination. Representations of the human
figure are common throughout the world. They have been found in all the
ancient civilizations, Asia Minor, Egypt, Greece and Rome, as well as among the
more primitive peoples such as some African tribes, Australian aborigines, Red Indians
and Eskimos. Before this age of mass production, of course, all dolls were made by hand.
They can often provide a key to the dress of a period or country, and to the maker's
personality. Unfortunately their fragility makes them difficult to preserve for any time.

They are delightful things to make and the more complex dolls need quite a high
degree of skill. You can almost feel them coming alive and imbued with the characters
that the maker chooses to give them. Sometimes however they develop along their
own lines and grow in a certain way in spite of the maker's efforts to control them. Sometimes even the toymaker's own personality becomes mixed with that of the doll under
construction. However, it still remains that handmade dolls have a personality and
individuality that mass-produced ones never will have in spite of their pretty faces and
curls. Dolls are things which one can lavish affection on when young and enjoy making
when older. You can make them for playthings or for their purely decorative qualities.
Apart from its being much more exciting to make one's own dolls, you are able to provide
your children with the dolls they prefer, dressed as they want them to be dressed, and
in the colours they love.

For the main part I have included dolls stitched from fabric. They start from the
simplest tube shape which a very young child could make, and work up to a more complex
jointed doll. This however is not really difficult. Many kinds of fabric can be used,
but the most convenient to handle is felt or firm cotton. Fabrics which slip or stretch
are more difficult to manage. Flesh-coloured material can be bought quite easily, but
you could dye calico to any shade you liked. The texture of the fabrics should be smooth
and have a close weave. When cutting out the different pattern sections see that the
grain is straight, so that the body and limbs can be stuffed straight.

No matter how simple the doll I think it is best to decide on a specific character
before you begin, even though it might be as vague as " this is going to be a merry doll
or a sad doll ". You will derive much pleasure both from creating the character or
expression and choosing the appropriate dress. With the more complex doll you can
have greater variety. For instance you may decide to make a schoolgirl, an Indian Prince,
an Elizabethan lady and so on.

TUBE OR PEG-SHAPED DOLLS

The simplest shape is a tube or peg shape. Try it in felt first. Cut two shapes, sew

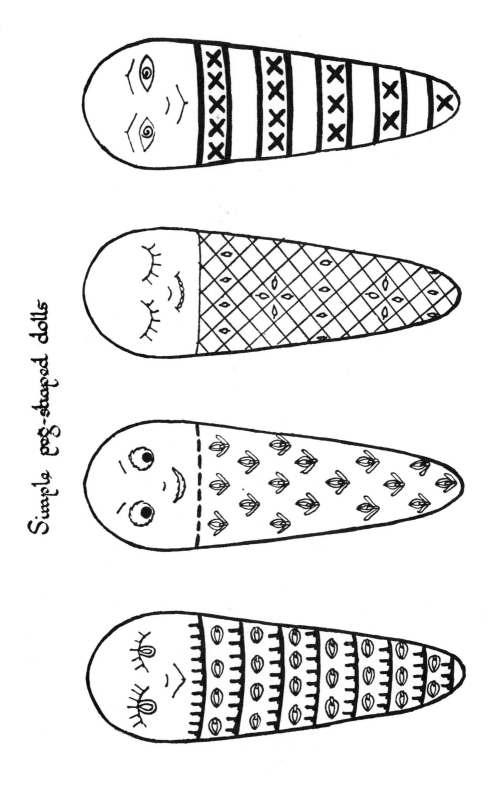

Simple peg-shaped dolls

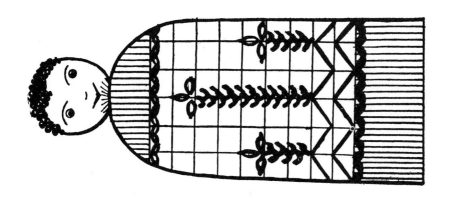

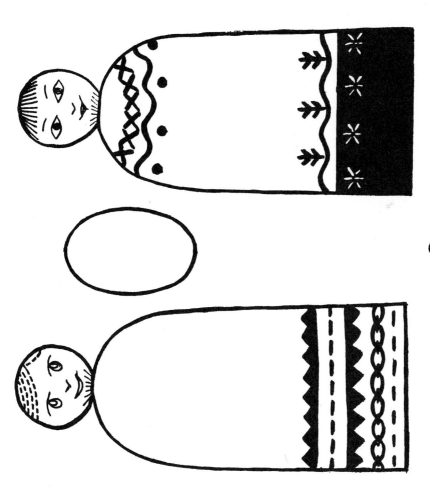

Some more standing dolls

them round with fishbone, stuff firmly and then embroider the lower end of the tube with simple stitches in thick cotton.   Stitches such as running, chain, buttonhole and varieties of running.   Work a simple face on the wide end of the tube, using buttonhole for the lashes, detached chain for the eyes, straight stitch for the nose and a single fly stitch for the mouth.   Other ways of decoration are shown in the diagram on page 158. The second tube has a running stitch dividing head from body, which is spotted with chain and fly stitch.   You could perhaps make this one in black and have a third yellow, and a fourth brown.   The second one also has stem stitch and French knots for the eyes, straight stitch for the eyebrows, and a shaped stem stitch mouth.

The third and fourth tubes have two different materials, a plain and patterned joined together.   Join the fabrics before cutting the shape.   Then cut the shapes in paper and cover these with the fabric, making sure that the join comes in the correct position.   If you have checked or striped material you can make the pattern the basis of your embroidery.   Once again use simple stitching for the face.   Little hats or caps often make these tube dolls more amusing and interesting.

TUBE DOLLS WITH SEPARATE HEADS

The next stage is to put a separate head on the tube shape (see page 161).   Cut the tube to the same size and make it up in the same way.   Draw and embroider a simple design on the body section.   The head is a circle of plain fabric.   Turn in the edges all round and run a gathering thread round.   Stuff the circle and pull up the gathering thread firmly.   Fasten off and stitch the head on to the broad end of the tube.   Fine fabric is best for the head so that it will gather well.   Work a simple face on to the knob. A few straight stitches from the centre top could be arranged to suggest hair.

CONE-SHAPED DOLLS

We now come on to the cone-shaped doll.   This will stand up.   It is like the Three Kings described in the section on Christmas decorations.

It is easiest made in felt.   If you use other fabrics remember to mount them on paper first.   Cut the side piece and work on your design, perhaps a piece of appliqué or a simple pattern made from cut paper shapes.   Sew along the back to join it.   Then sew in the circle for the base, having first fitted in a piece of card so that it will be flat. A tiny motif on the base would make a good finish.   The whole thing is stuffed from the top.   Then make a head in the same way as for the previous doll.   Sew it into position over the hole in the top of the cone.

STANDING DOLLS WITH OVAL BASE

The next shape (page 159) is also based on the tube shape, but like the cone it will stand, this time on an oval base.   There is also a slight shoulder line.   You will need two shapes which are seamed together.   Then fit in the base over a piece of card.   Stitch about half-way round.   Stuff the shape and finish sewing in the base.

Many kinds of decoration may be used.   In the diagram the first figure has strips of pinked felt allied with varieties of running stitch.   The next has two contrasting fabrics with a little simple embroidery on each, while the third has two patterned fabrics joined so that there are stripes above and below a checked centre piece.   When using more

Peg and cone-shaped dolls
with separate heads

Base

than one material do see that the joins are level on both sides, so that when the back and front shapes are sewn together there is no break in the line. The heads are made in the same way as those for the cone and tube. A little hair can be embroidered on them : straight stitches coming from the centre in a fairly thick cotton, or French knots worked closely giving the appearance of curls, or rows of running stitch.

BARREL-SHAPED DOLLS

The egg- or barrel-shaped dolls on page 163 are similar to the previous ones. This time they stand on a small circular base, once again stiffened with card. Try using different fabrics. The first in the diagram has a single embroidered motif worked on an applied shape. The next body is made from striped fabric enriched with rows of running stitch. In this case the stripes have been cut on the cross and joined down the centre so that they make a V shape. The spotted fabric has a design round the spots. One can suggest simple clothing by stitchery, a coat or blouse as in the third diagram. You could also work arms or sleeves in stitchery if you wished. The heads are the gathered and stuffed circles of material as described earlier. Those in the diagram have tiny felt crowns with a little fine embroidery. Other small hats would look well provided they are in keeping both in size and shape with the body. These dolls would make delightful decorations, especially if they were made in rich fabric and worked with more elaborate stitching. You could make quite a feature of the head-dress.

SHAPED TUBE DOLLS—A KING AND QUEEN

The shaped tube dolls on page 164 are a little more difficult in construction. They also need very neat sewing. For a beginning use fabric which is firm and does not easily fray. You can of course make any character you choose. The clothing, which is worked on the doll itself, must come to the ground. There are no feet, but the arms are made separately and stitched on after the body is finished.

The man is the easier shape so I would advise starting with him. Join two pieces of fabric together on the wrong side, the top piece suitable for the face and the bottom for the clothing. Then cut out the paper shapes, one each for the back and front. Place them on the joined material so that the join between the face and body comes in the right place. Cut round, leaving a turning, and tack over the paper in the usual way. Then work any embroidery necessary on the face and clothing. Use very fine thread for the features so that they do not appear heavy or clumsy.

Sew the back and front together and stuff gently but firmly. Then sew in the base with a piece of card inside. The hair can now be worked. The diagram shows clusters of French knots worked very closely. Make the arms in the same way as the body, joining the fabric first, for the hand and sleeve, and then making the stitchery. Neatly seam the two sections together, stuff and carefully sew them into position on the body round the top of the shoulder.

The Queen is a little more difficult in shape. She has four different fabrics in her make-up. These should be carefully measured before joining so that they are in proportion when you come to cover the paper shapes. If the material is patterned do see that it is small enough in scale to suit the size of the doll.

Base

Barrel shaped
dolls with
separate heads

Dolls made from
shaped tubes
with separate arms

Base for
Queen

Base for
King

Work your embroidery and join the two sections together, seeing that the seams between the different materials meet exactly. Fit in the oval base and stuff gently. The hair is worked straight on to the head. Mark the shape of the hair in pencil first. Suitable stitches are whipped running coral knots, twisted chain, whipped chain or threaded backstitch. Keep the rows very even and quite close. Various coiffures may be devised. Double herringbone is useful for suggesting a plait. Make the arms in the same way as those for the King.

This type of doll looks quite well with the addition of a little loose clothing, such as cloaks, crowns, hats, head-dresses. Be sure that it is on the same scale as the doll. A bride with her train and coronet, or a nurse with apron and cap, would be attractive.

These tube dolls may be varied in shape. If you make the whole doll in flesh-coloured fabric, it is a simple matter to sew on clothing, perhaps a fitted bodice, and then several petticoats topped by a skirt. They should be the full length of the doll, however, as there are no feet. The arms are made separately, tubes as before, but with a little shaping or bend in them. Add the sleeves and then sew on to the doll. An extra face may be added and separate hair as that described further on for the larger dolls.

WIRE OR PIPE-CLEANER DOLLS: THE BALLET

In some doll shapes a wire is necessary, so I have included a diagram of the shape (page 166). Pipe-cleaners or any soft pliable wires are good for this. You will need a length for the head and body, and a length each for the arms and legs. It is fun sometimes to dress up the wire just as it is with fine muslin or soft paper bodices and ballet skirts. Interesting groups of figures can be composed as the wire bends very easily. If you wish the figures to stand permanently as for a theatre set, a little Sellotape over the feet will fix them to the floor. A large wooden bead could be used for the head, threaded on to the wire before the twisting, or even a little clay, modelled on to the wire head shape. Hands and feet could be modelled too if necessary.

SHAPED DOLL WITH ARMS AND LEGS

The next doll shape (page 167) has arms and legs cut in one with the body. Made in felt this shape is quite substantial, but if it is in a lighter fabric, pipe-cleaners give it a better finish. These should be put in before the doll is stuffed. Stuff each arm from the hand, and each leg from the foot. The pipe-cleaners enable the doll's arms and legs to be bent a little into different positions. The shape would be good made from a woollen stocking, larger of course. A black one would make a golliwog or black mammy doll.

Joints can be made in this shape with one or two rows of machine stitching along the tops of the arms and legs. There would be no pipe-cleaners in this case.

Unless you make a large doll I would advise stitching the clothing on to the body and keeping it to very simple shapes—squares and rectangles are best. Shoes can be put on this doll if they are made separately. Stuff the toe and put the end of the doll's leg into the heel, stuffing round it until the shoe is full. Finish by stitching the leg into the shoe.

DOLLS' FACES

The larger doll needs more complex stitchery for the face. You will find some ways

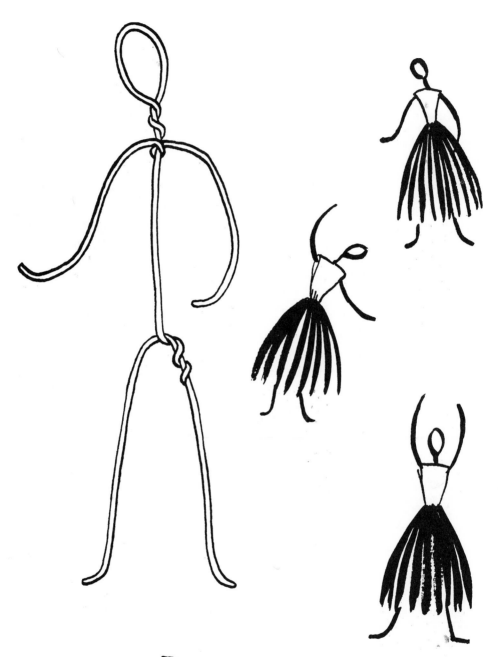

Pipe-cleaner dolls

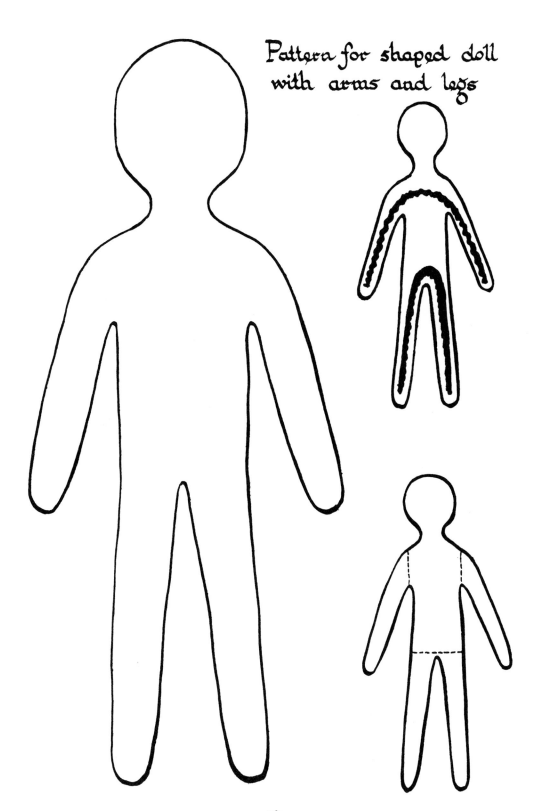

Pattern for shaped doll
with arms and legs

illustrated on page 169. As a general rule use very fine thread. If it is too thick the features are ugly and often out of proportion. A simple face has buttonhole for the eye-lashes and solid chain in two colours for the eyes, the lighter colour on the outside.

Another type of face has applied pieces of fabric. Felt is good, provided it is fairly thin. There being no edges to turn under, embroidery added to the applied shapes often improves them. It is a simple matter to cut different shapes for features in paper first. Try round, almond-shaped, oval or triangular eyes. Beads, buttons and rings may be useful too. Projecting beads however are not suitable for young children. By moving the pupil in the eye you can have different expressions. The eyes are usually about half-way down the head.

The patterns for these cloth dolls all include a flat face, but a projecting face giving a chin may be added. When the body is stuffed cut a circle slightly larger than the head, and sew two small darts at the bottom edge. The distance between these darts determines the width of the chin. Then turn under the raw edge of the circle and pin it in position from where the ear would come round the jawline up to the second ear. Hem along this edge with matching thread. Then run a gathering thread round the top edge of the circle, turning in the raw edge as before. Stuff the space between the first and second faces firmly, and pull the gathering thread up until the edge fits round the top of the head. Sew this in position. The gathers will be hidden when hair is added.

By fine stem stitching and using several shades of thread a face with more character is possible. One can add a little shading under the eyes, in the bend of the chin, round the nose and at the corners of the eyes. This stitching must needs be very delicate. A shading in the mouth can be suggested by filling in the top lip with a darker shade than that used for the bottom one. A few simple lines drawn on the face with a very sharp pencil are helpful at the beginning. You can of course put more darts round the jaw line to vary the shape of the face.

DOLLS' HAIR

The hair may differ in colour, shape and texture. For smaller dolls use finer thread. All manner of materials are useful for hair : wool, silk, cottons of various thicknesses and textures, rug wool, weaving cottons, felt, leather, raffia, etc. Try to make the hair both in style and texture in keeping with the character of the doll.

Felt or leather hair is stitched on to the head in tiers (page 170). Fringe the appropriate lengths of felt, using a fine one, and sew the underneath layer on first. Then the fringe, the middle layer and finally the last one which will meet down the middle to form a parting. A little chain or stem stitching along the parting improves the look of it.

A curly head is simple too. Wind your wool round a pencil or skewer, the thickness of which determines the size of the curl, for about $1\frac{1}{2}''$ (diagram on page 170). Then stem stitch firmly in a matching thread along one side, drawing the wool together. When you reach the end, slip the curl off the pencil and stitch on to the doll. You will find that the curl springs up quite naturally. Sew the curls on fairly close together to give a nice mop.

Plaits are comparatively easy to make. First of all cover in the back of the head with a strip of hair. Measure the depth needed from the top of the head to the nape of the

PLATE 7

PLATE 8

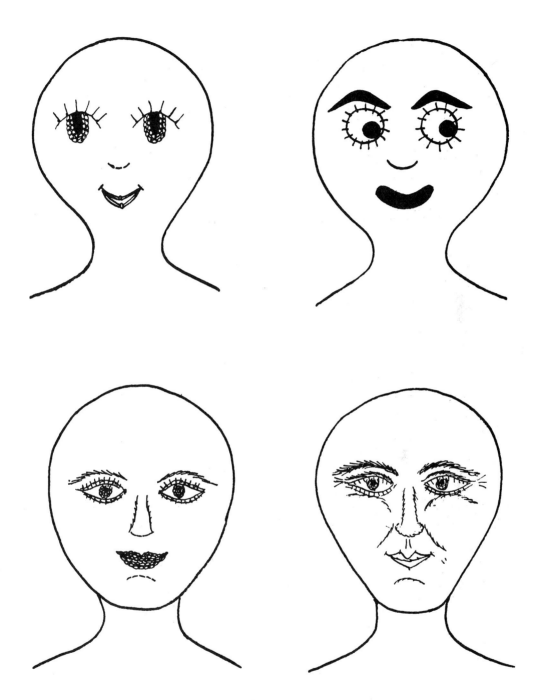

Some ways of working doll faces

Fringed and curled
hair

Two ways of
arranging plaited
hair

neck.   Cut a piece of card to this depth and wind your wool round it, gently and without stretching.   You may have to go backwards and forwards once or twice so that the hair is quite thick.   Too little wool looks thin and scraggy and does not cover the head properly.   Make certain you wind a sufficient length—roughly the distance from ear to ear. Then stem stitch firmly along the top and bottom (upper diagram on page 171).   Slide the hair off the card and sew it in position.

Now make the top hair and plaits.   Use the same method.   This time you will need a longer and narrower strip of card.   Remember that the plaiting takes up quite a lot of hair and allow for it.   Stem stitch along the top only and cut along the bottom (lower diagram on page 171).   Open out the hair and fit over the top of the head with the seam in the middle.   Stitch at the back and front.   Plait the ends and stitch the tops of the plaits to the head, making certain that all the skull is covered.   You may have to put an odd stitch in here and there to keep the hair in shape round the face.

More elaborate coiffures may be devised with the combined use of strips of hair, plaits and curls.   The fourth diagram on page 171 shows a coil of hair in a bun on top of the head.   It is made from raffia.   This is a good medium for hair as the dye is sometimes mixed and there is a certain gloss on it.   It does need very careful stitching, however, because of the splitting.   The main strip of hair is made like the back of the plaited style.   You will need enough to wrap right round the head, the top seam meeting in the middle.   Then make a long plait.   Sew it on, starting at the top of the head.   Come down the centre back, round below the ear, across the front of the head, round the other ear and back up the centre back, finishing off with a bun made of coils of the plait piled on top of one another.   This bun will cover the starting point.   Finish by pushing the end inside the coils and stitching firmly.   Coils at the sides of the head or the nape of the neck, both round and oval, look well.

Short hair made of raffia is effective.   Wind the raffia round a card as described earlier.   Stitch very firmly along the top, cut along the lower edge.   Then sew on to the doll, making the stitching form the centre parting.   Catch the two ends down at the back so that the back of the head is covered.   Fringe the raffia finely by splitting it down with a needle.

JOINTED DOLLS

I have included three dolls with separate arms and legs.   The first (page 173) makes up into a long slim doll rather like the old wooden " Betty ".   Cut each piece from double material, having two arm and two leg sections.   It is best to draw round each piece on the wrong side of the fabric and then cut round, leaving a turning.   Machine or backstitch on the pencil line.   Leave open the straight edge along the bottom of the body and the top of each arm, and both top and bottom of the leg.   Cut the turnings fairly close and clip to the seam where there are curves—at the neck, waist and ankle.

Turn all the pieces on to the right side.   Stuff the body firmly, turn in the turning left at the bottom and seam neatly across.   Stuff the arms to within 1″ of the top.   Then backstitch across.   Turn in the ends and seam.   This gives a flat piece at the top of the arm which serves as a hinge or joint.   Make the soles of the feet by cutting the sole shape in card and tacking a piece of fabric over it.   Fold in the turning round the foot, fit the

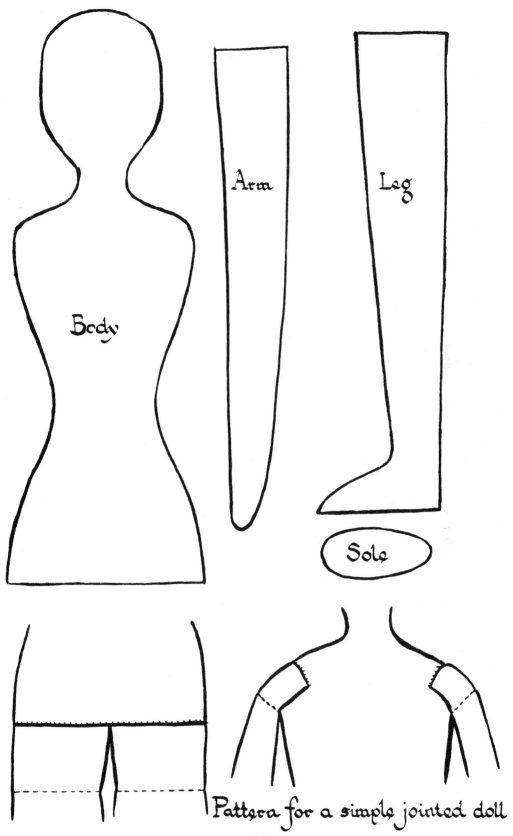

Body

Arm

Leg

Sole

Pattern for a simple jointed doll

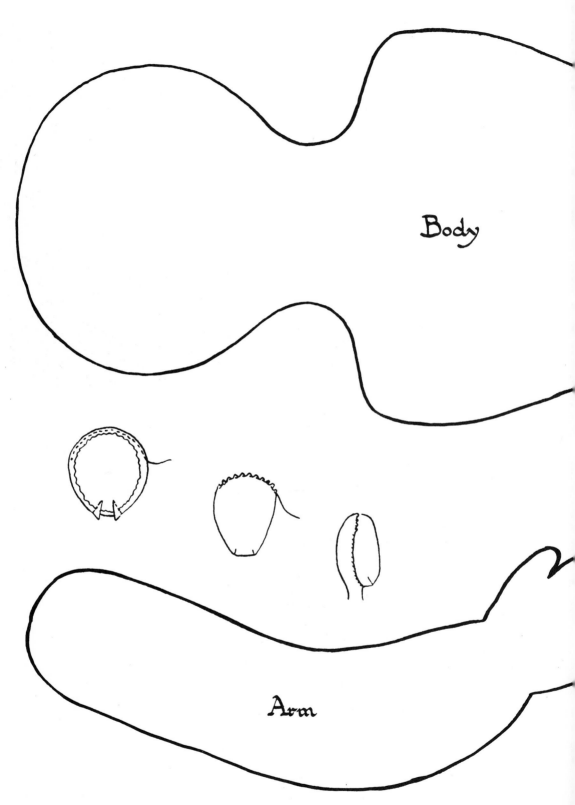

Body

Arm

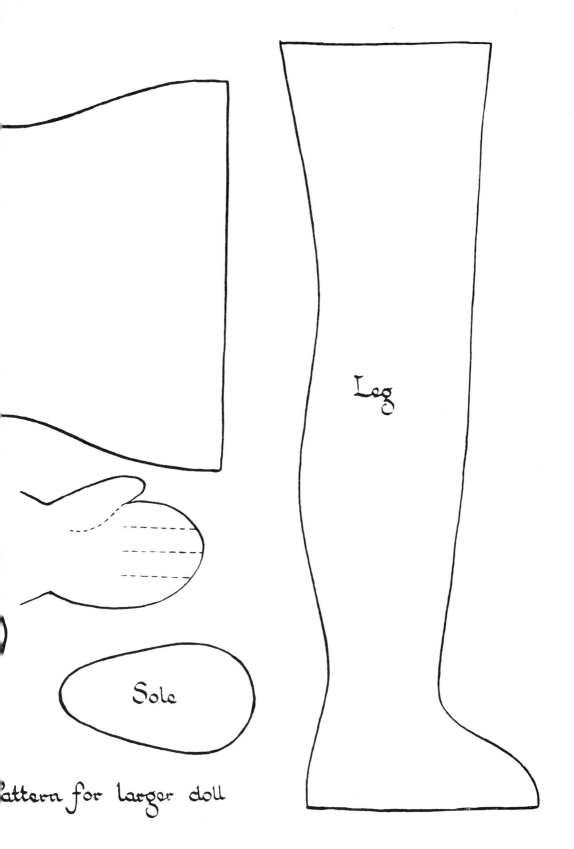

Leg

Sole

attern for larger doll

175

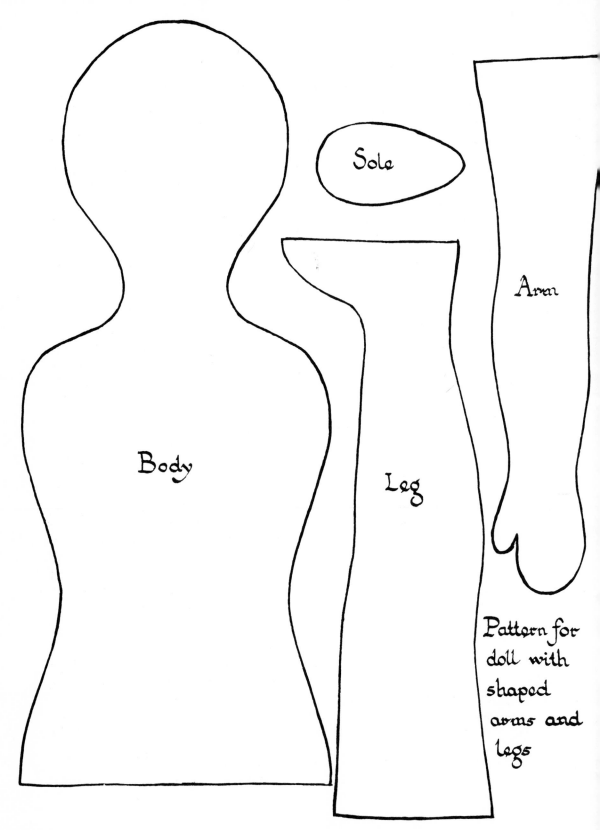

Body

Sole

Arm

Leg

Pattern for
doll with
shaped
arms and
legs

sole into the space and seam it into position. Then stuff again to within an inch of the top. Backstitch across, remembering that the seams on the leg run down the centre front and back and not down the sides. Turn in the ends of the legs and finish off.

Sew the arms on to the shoulders, stitching across several times to make them secure. Sew the legs on to the lower edge of the body. Embroider the face and then make and fit the hair. Further joints at the elbows and knees may be made by stuffing only up to the elbows and then making two rows of backstitching with a small space between, thus forming a hinge.

Both the medium and large dolls (pages 174–6) are made in the way described earlier. A flat hand looks better on the large doll. Put a little stuffing in the hand and spread it out evenly. Then make rows of saddle stitch down the hand, dividing it into fingers. Use a matching thread, pulling it quite tight. Stitch in a line for the thumb also. Then continue stuffing as usual.

DOLLS' CLOTHES—FABRICS, FITTING, FASTENINGS

Keep all your pieces from fur and leather to organdie and brocades, all your beads, sequins, feathers, braids, etc., for dressing your dolls. Dolls' clothes require quite a high degree of neatness and skilful sewing if they are to be successful. It is essential that the seams are fine and delicate and not clumsy. They naturally come close together in some garments, so if they are very bulky the whole shape of the garment is lost and the shape of the doll hidden. The larger dolls need quite large pieces of fabric; one must be careful with the grain of the material. Small skimped clothes look ill-fitting and are always difficult to fasten. Consequently they are soon worn with constant putting on and taking off. Do see that armholes are big enough to take the fattest part of the arm, also that placket openings are long enough.

The scale of pattern and decoration is very important. On no account have a fabric with a large pattern for a small doll. The whole thing is out of proportion. The same rule applies for stitches, thickness of thread, braids, cords, etc. Do see that they are scaled down to fit in with the size of the doll. Fastenings must be just as tiny and dainty too. On the whole I find tiny hooks and buttonhole bars the most satisfactory. If the doll is for a child, small hand-made buttons and buttonholes might be better. Knitting for vests, jumpers, socks, etc., should also be fine enough to look in proportion with the doll. Fine wool or cotton, and sometimes even hatpins, are necessary to give the correct tension.

ATTACHED CLOTHES—FOR PEASANT GIRL DOLL

So far the dolls have had stitching on the shape, suggesting clothing, or the shape made of different fabrics enriched with embroidery, also serving for the clothing. The next stage is to sew separate garments on to the doll. These are loose except at the points of attachment, but they cannot be taken off. For the smaller dolls it is much the better method. If the garments are very tiny a number of openings and fastenings only make them clumsy.

The small thin doll described on page 172 is dressed (page 179) in pieces of fabric which are all simple in shape, mainly rectangles. Cut two rectangles of white fabric, about 5″ wide and as long as you wish, for the knickers.   Use something fine, such as lawn.   Fold each rectangle in half and sew about half-way up.   Now sew the two legs together.   Run a gathering thread round the waist without turning in any edges. Turn under the edges of the legs once and tack round a length of lace.   Run a gathering thread through both lawn and lace.   Slip the knickers on to the doll and draw up all the gathers.   Space them evenly, then stitch the garment on to the doll round the waist and legs.

The petticoat is a rectangle of fabric measuring 17″ × 6″.   Make a fine French seam along the short ends.   Turn under a small hem round one of the long edges.   This looks attractive with a little fine embroidery.   Use only one thread of cotton.   Gather the waist and fit on to the doll.   The figure in the diagram has a long-waisted dress, so the top of the petticoat is about an inch below the waist.   Pull the gathers into position and once more stitch on to the doll.

The skirt of the dress is made to the same measurements as the petticoat.   In the original it is a bronze-coloured silk with an embroidered scallop design along the bottom worked in single threads of white, blue, black, lemon, pink and turquoise.   Gather the waist and stitch it over the petticoat.

Cut two rectangles of fabric for the bodice, sufficiently long and wide to fit one side of the doll.   Fold in the top and bottom edges and pin to the doll from neck to lower bodice edge.   Make the lower edge fit over the top of the skirt gathers, thus hiding the raw edge.   Fold the corners of the back bodice over the shoulders and the sides round to the front.   You may have to clip the sides to give a good fit with no wrinkles across the back.   Stitch all these edges on to the doll.   Neatly hem along the lower folded edge.

Now put on the front part of the bodice, cutting the edges to shape and turning them in so that they overlap the back bodice across the shoulders and down the sides.   Turn in the lower edge also and fit over the skirt gathers.   Neatly hem all these seams with matching thread.   The only raw edges now are those round the armholes.

The embroidery on the bodice is worked directly on to it.   Draw your design on with a very sharp pencil.   This doll has a blue bodice worked with black, lemon, red and white.   The thread is fine and the stitches small.

The sleeves are in two sections.   Cut the full top section from fine white material about 5″ × 3½″.   Down the centre make a loop design in red and black.   Join the sides. Fold the top edge under and gather so that it fits the shoulder.   Slip on the doll and sew into position.   Gather the lower edge and pull up to fit the arm.   Stitch this on to the doll also.   Make the long narrow cuff from the blue bodice fabric.   Fold in top and bottom edges.   Place the top edge over the gathers of the top sleeve section and have the lower edge in position at the wrist.   Hem with matching thread and sew on to the doll.   Fold in the raw edge down the outside of the arm and hem that also.   The outside seam has a row of tiny white beads along it with fine red buttonhole stitch on each side.

The slippers are of blue felt.   Seam the backs together, then place on the foot and sew on the sole.   There is a little red and lemon embroidery both on the top and sole. Make the plantpot hat from red felt and work a fine border in black, white and turquoise. There is a black and lemon motif on the front (patterns p. 181).   Try other designs and costumes but keep the shapes simple with all raw edges firmly stitched out of sight.

Examples of clothing stitched onto the doll

ATTACHED CLOTHES—FOR MOORISH DOLL

The medium-sized doll also has the clothing stitched on. However if the shapes are kept simple it can be fairly easily made separately.

The doll in the diagram on page 179 is made of black poplin with features of felt appliqué. The hair is black wool curls. Make the baggy trousers from two pieces of fabric $8\frac{1}{2}''$ square. Choose something gay. The original has green and white striped organza with a gold thread in it. Fold each piece in half and sew together for the length of the leg. Then stitch the two legs together. Gather round the waist and bottom of the leg, slip on to the doll and draw up the threads to fit. Stitch firmly on to the doll's body. Sew the bottom of the legs a little way up from the ankle, to allow for a piece of finishing braid.

Cut the blouse from yellow silk—two squares, wider than the width of the body to allow for gathering. Fold a box pleat down the middle of the front and fasten it down with blue running stitch. Sew small blue sequins along the centre of the pleat—they serve as buttons. Join the back and front pieces as far as the underarm. Gather the lower edge. Put it on the doll, pull up the gathers and sew over the trouser edge. Slightly hollow the neck of both back and front pieces. Gather the front across the shoulders and sew into position. Fold under the edges of the shoulders on the back and lap them over the front, hiding the raw edges. Seam them into position with matching thread. Gather the fullness left across the back neck and stitch on to the doll.

Make a standing collar by folding a piece of fabric to a width of half an inch and long enough to go round the neck with a little overlap. Fold the end to a point. Sew round the neck with blue running stitches with a sequin on the end of the point. A further decoration is a strip of bronze ric-rac braid sewn along the centre of the collar.

Cut two pieces of silk $6'' \times 5''$ for the sleeves. The six inches is the width. Fold in half and seam together on the wrong side. Turn under the top edge, gather and sew on to the bodice round the armhole. Gather the lower edge and sew on to the wrist. Finish off the cuffs at wrist and ankle with strips of $\frac{1}{2}''$ blue and white braid, sewing firmly on to the doll and enclosing all the raw edges. Tie a sash of red chiffon round the waist. You could even make a card scimitar and fasten it into the sash.

The bolero is cut from the given pattern (page 181) and made in green felt. The edge is finished with silver beading sewn on with red thread. The rest of the border decoration is a line of small dark beads, a row of white running, black coral knot and finally red single fly stitch.

The turban is a coil wound round and round like a shell. Cut a long strip of fabric on the cross—that in the diagram is red, white and gold striped organza—and wrap it round a rolled strip of wadding, stitching it along. Then make a small green felt cone and stitch it to the top of the doll's head. Coil the roll of striped fabric round the head, building the coils on top of each other, finishing so that part of the felt cone shows from the top. Pin in position first and then catch stitch the rolls together and on to the head. Cover the lines of sewing with a couched gold thread. The turban is finished with a little bunch of pink and silver-headed stamens sewn at the side, the stitching being covered with three blue sequins. Two loops of beads, one bronze and one white, are sewn at each side of the head for ear-rings.

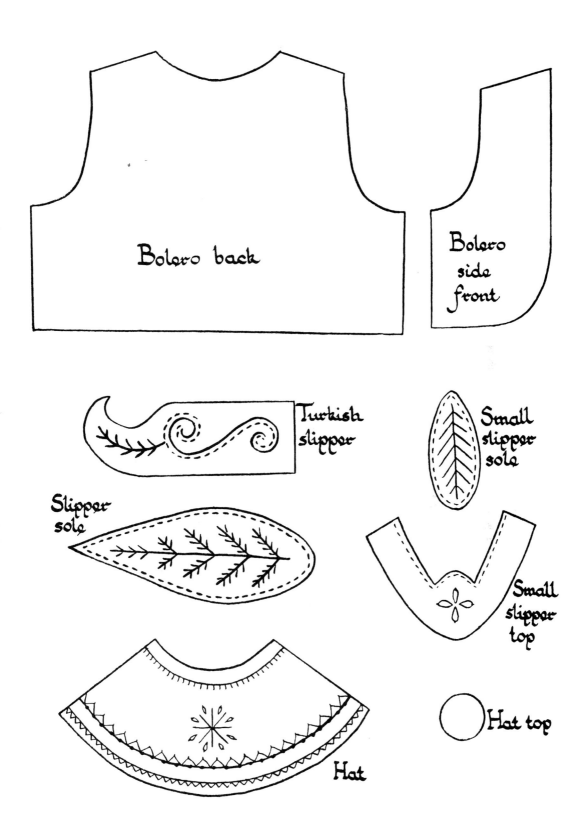

Bolero back

Bolero side front

Turkish slipper

Small slipper sole

Slipper sole

Small slipper top

Hat

Hat top

181

Cut the curly-toed shoes from the pattern. They are red felt decorated with black, blue and yellow embroidery. Sew them together with matching thread, then work a small white buttonhole stitch over the seam between the sole and the upper.

DETACHABLE CLOTHING

We now come to clothing which can be taken off the doll. I have included several patterns of blouses, skirts, bodices, etc. These styles may be varied by combining different types of sleeve, collar and so on. None of these patterns have any turnings allowed, so you must remember to add them when cutting out. Allow $\frac{1}{8}''$ for single seams and $\frac{1}{4}''$ for double ones such as the French seams used for sides, shoulders and skirt seams. Allow $\frac{1}{4}''$ also for hems, except for those at the bottom where you will use your own judgment. Much depends on the weight of the fabric and the type of hem. A French seam is sewn first on the right side and then on the wrong. Keep the seams as narrow and as neat as possible, avoiding bulky materials as much as you can.

KNICKERS

There are three knicker patterns on page 183—a long one for a Victorian doll, a shorter one for a more modern doll, and a pilch pattern for a baby doll. To make the knickers cut two shapes like the pattern, each from double fabric with a fold down the long straight side. Lawn is very good for dolls' underwear, being fine and comparatively easy to handle.

Make a French seam along the curved edges, joining together the two sections back and front. Then make a second French seam along the short straight leg sides, also joining the two sections. Fold a hem round the top wide enough to take narrow slotting elastic and machine it down, leaving an open space in which to thread the elastic. Turn under a similar hem round each leg, sewing it in the same way. If you are trimming the legs with lace sew it on now, stitching it to the edge of the fold. Make the join come on the inside of the leg. Finally slot the elastic into the legs and the top. You can measure the quantity by stretching your elastic round the widest parts of the doll's body, and allowing a little extra for joining. Join elastic by overlapping the two ends flatly and seaming round the four sides of the overlap. The shorter knickers are made in exactly the same way.

When you cut the pilch pattern, have the fold along the short straight line at the bottom. Use a French seam for the sides and a hem with elastic slotted in for the top. The legs have no elastic but are finished with a very narrow crossway binding—that is, cut a narrow strip of fabric on the bias, place the edge of the strip to the edge of the pilch leg right sides together. Using a running stitch sew them together along the edges, join the two ends of the binding with a seam also cut on the cross. Fold the bias strip over to the wrong side, turn under the edge and hem to the line of running stitches, which will have come through to the wrong side.

PETTICOATS

The petticoat (page 184) may have a bodice and skirt or skirt only. If the doll has very full outer garments, two or more petticoats are better—one with the bodice and the

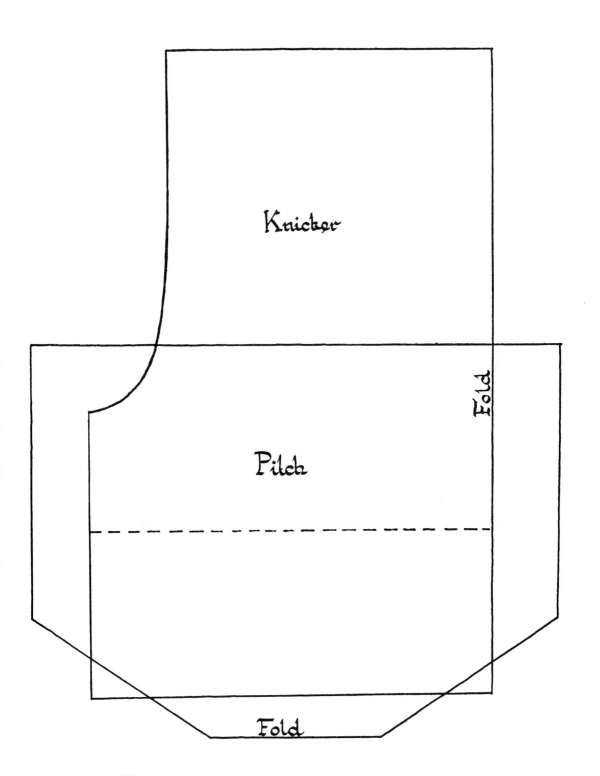

Knicker

Fold

Pilch

Fold

Knicker and pilch patterns

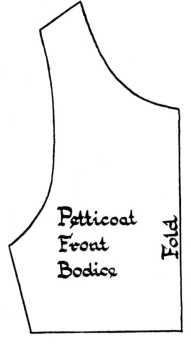

Petticoat
Front
Bodice

Fold

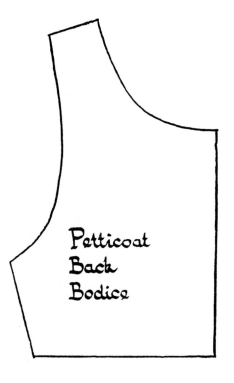

Petticoat
Back
Bodice

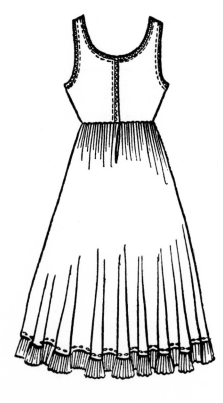

Pattern for petticoat
and waist slip

others with just the skirt. You could have a flannel waist petticoat with a lawn one on top. If you do use a woollen fabric choose something smooth and fine. The waist slip of course is just a straight length of material joined up the side with a French seam. You will cut it to any length you wish, remembering to allow extra for the hem. Leave a space open at the top of the seam for a placket. You can if you wish make a proper placket opening by sewing on a straight strip of material and turning it over to a hem on the wrong side. Sometimes, however, it is easier and less bulky just to clip the turning of the French seam and make a tiny hem along both sides of the opening.

Gather along the top edge of the petticoat. Cut a strip of fabric on the straight, long enough to go round the doll's waist fairly tightly with a little left over for turnings and overlap. Remember that this strip is to be folded in half, so do not have it too narrow. Pull up the gathers on the skirt so that they fit the waistband, leaving a little extra at one end for the waistband turning and a little more than this at the other end for the lap-over of the band. Space the gathers evenly, stroking them if necessary, and with the right sides of both band and skirt facing each other, backstitch or machine along, turning in the side edges of the band and seaming them neatly. Fasten with a buttonhole bar and hook—this latter on the extra piece projecting on the band. Do see that the skirt fits the doll firmly and remember to have plenty of material so that it does not look skimped. Then it will make a better basis for the outer garments.

The bodice is joined at the sides and shoulders with a French seam. Turn in a hem at the edges of the centre back. Face the armholes and neck with crossway strips. These hems and facings look attractive if they are sewn down with a fine coloured running stitch. Further delicate decoration may be added—such as buttonhole, vandyke buttonhole, feather stitch, etc. Make a skirt for this petticoat as already described. Make an opening at the top of the joining seam, gather the waist and fit on to the bodice. With the right sides together, backstitch the bodice and skirt together. Trim the seam closely and cover it with a crossway binding. No raw edges should now be visible.

The bottom hems can be finished off in a variety of ways—plain sewing or an embroidery stitch such as whipped or threaded running. Further embroidery will enrich the border. Lace or frilling looks attractive, and tiers of frilling look very elegant indeed, especially under a full skirt. If you finish the hem with scallops or points, make sure that they are small enough to look dainty and in proportion with the doll. No doubt other ways of making underslips will occur to you. Cut the patterns in paper first and try them on the doll before making them in fabric.

BLOUSES

The blouse patterns all have the same bodice shape, but you can vary the styles with different sleeves and collars. The fastenings on the diagrams are at the front but there is no reason why they should not be at the back.

For the blouse on page 186, cut the fabric with a fold down the centre back. The front is in two pieces. If you wish to put a different piece on the front as there is in the diagram, cut it now, not forgetting to leave the turnings on. Sew each piece on to each front shape and then turn in the hems down the centre front. Make French seams at the shoulders and sides.

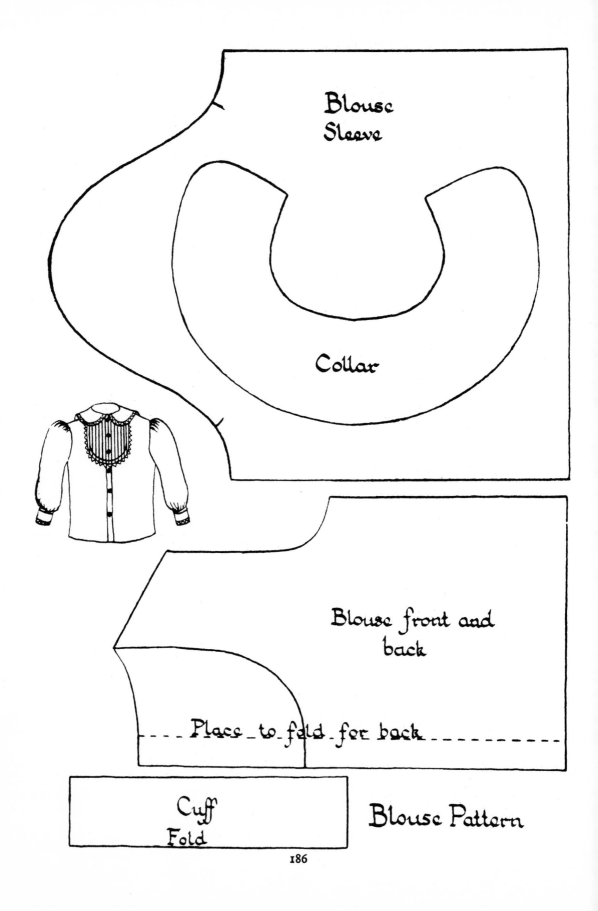

Blouse
Sleeve

Collar

Blouse front and
back

Place to fold for back

Cuff
Fold

Blouse Pattern

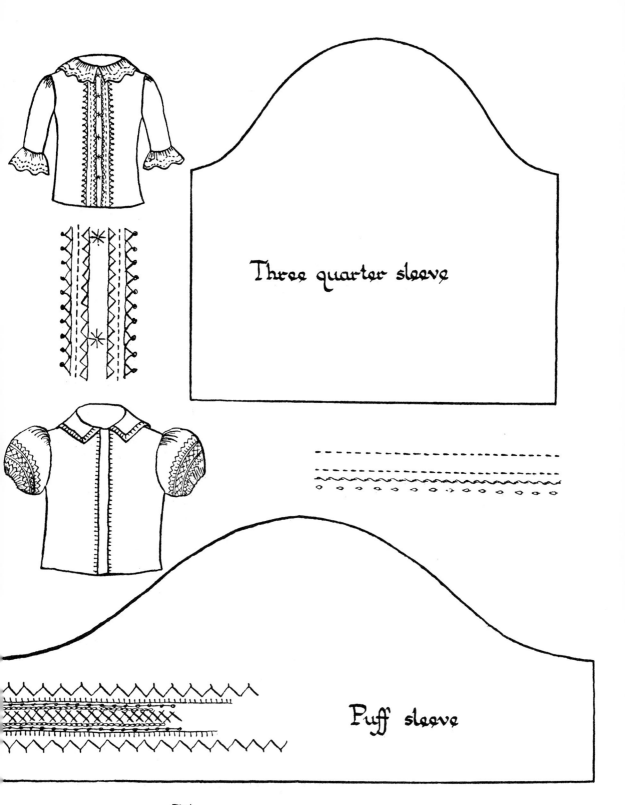

Three quarter sleeve

Puff sleeve

Two sleeve patterns

Now make the sleeves. Sew the sides with a French seam, leaving an opening at the wrist end. Finish this off to form a placket. Cut the cuff sections. Gather the wrist edge of the sleeve and fit the gathers along the cuff, leaving the cuff turnings projecting at each end. Have the right sides facing and backstitch along. Fold the cuff over to the inside, turn under the hem and sew to the line of stitching which shows on the other side. Turn in the turnings at each end and seam them. Gather the top of the sleeve between the marks, and fit into the armhole. Space the gathers evenly and backstitch. Trim the seam and bind it with a crossway strip.

Cut the collar from double fabric and sew round the outside edge on the wrong side. Turn it out and fit it round the neck on the right side. Place a bias strip over the edge and sew through all the thicknesses—blouse neck, collar and bias strip. Turn the binding on to the wrong side and finish off with a hem. Sew small press fasteners or tiny hooks and buttonhole bars down the front and on the sleeve cuffs. Further decoration may be added in the form of embroidery round the collar, front and cuffs. Very small beads or sequins will serve as buttons.

A second sleeve (page 187) is a three-quarter length without the fullness of the previous one. The frill is a straight piece of fabric gathered to fit the sleeves. The collar is the same. Both are sewn on with bias strips of fabric. Very fine embroidery decorates the edges of the cuffs, collar and fronts. Work the embroidery before assembling the garment.

Then we have a puff sleeve. The blouse bodice is like the others. Sew the short sleeve seam with a French seam, turn under the hem—wide enough to take slotting elastic, and leave a place open for threading the elastic. Then work any decoration. Gather the top edge, sewing it into the armhole and finishing it off as before. Then slot in the elastic.

The collar is a straight piece of folded material which fits round the neck except for the overlap of the fronts. Join the two short ends of the collar on the wrong side. Turn it out and fit round the blouse neck on the right side. Backstitch the under section of the collar on to the bodice. Then turn the upper section edge over to the wrong side and hem it on to the line of stitching. The fronts of the blouse and collar edges are finished with small buttonhole stitch.

The last blouse shape (page 189) is made from rectangles with a little hollowing for the neck. Leave openings at the tops of the side seams for the armholes. The rectangular sleeves are made in the same way as those for the first blouse. Use the cuff pattern and gather the sleeve into it as before. Gather the tops and sew them into the armholes. These gathers are decorated with two bands of single fly stitch, a row of running and a row of buttonhole. The shoulder seams have a row of buttonhole on both sides pointing forward and back. The front piece is made separately from double fabric and stitched on to one of the blouse fronts, after it has been hemmed of course. Half of the pointed front will be sewn on to the blouse, the other half will stand off. This will fasten down on to the second front when the blouse is finished.

The collar is a straight piece of double material with rounded ends. It fits exactly round the neck. Sew it together on the wrong side and then turn it out. Sew it on to the blouse in the same way as for the straight collar. It is embroidered with chain,

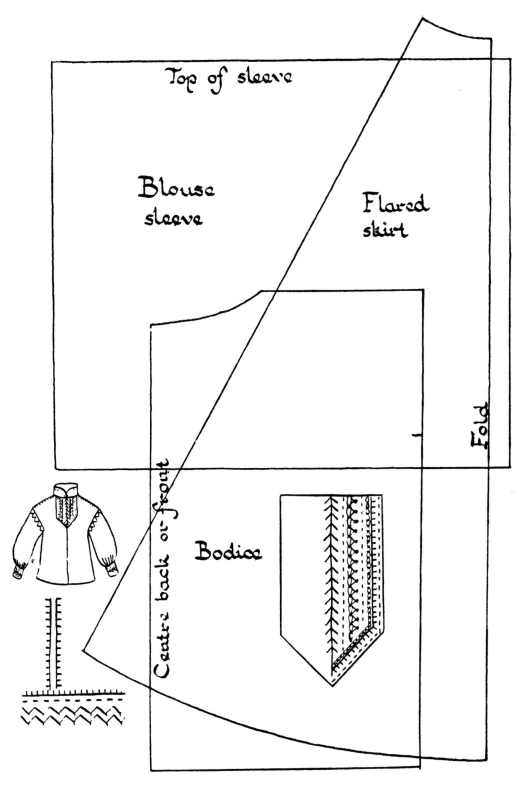

Top of sleeve

Blouse
sleeve

Flared
skirt

Fold

Centre back or front

Bodice

Patterns for blouse and flared skirt

189

buttonhole and running stitches along the outer edge.   The front and cuffs are heavily embroidered.   Round the outside edges there are running, buttonhole and chain.   There is fly stitch down the middle with running, crested chain and running again on each side of it.   The cuffs have a similar design.   Fasten the blouse with hooks and buttonhole bars, having one at the point of the decorated front with others at the top and bottom of the straight side of it.

SKIRTS

Gathered skirts are made like the waist slips.   Allow plenty of material to give a pleasant fullness.   The length is a matter of taste or style, but be careful not to have it too short.

The flared skirt pattern on page 189 is cut in four pieces all joined with French seams and then mounted on to a band.   A skirt with knife or box pleats could be made from a strip of straight fabric just as for the gathered skirt.   All manner of decorations are attractive—braids, bindings, embroidery, machine stitching, applied bands of material, as long as they are in proportion to the size of the garment.

BOLEROS AND WAISTCOATS

Very often a little jacket or bolero finishes off a blouse and skirt outfit.   If you are dressing your doll in costume they are sometimes essential.   Felt is a good fabric for beginners to use.   It cuts easily and there are no small awkward turnings.   If however you make your jackets of material that frays, use a fine fabric for a lining.   This is cut to the same pattern and all the raw edges are then enclosed inside.   Do not forget to clip here and there on curved edges so that there is no puckering.   Gay and pretty linings can enhance a jacket as well as making it more substantial.

I have suggested some designs for stitchery on the actual pattern shapes on page 191. Work the embroidery before making up the waistcoat.   It is fastened at the waist with a hook and bar.   Made in black and worn over a white blouse with a vivid skirt it looks delightful.   The bolero is useful for gypsy or golliwog dolls.   Beads and sequins enrich it.   If you make it in felt use fishbone stitch for the seams.   They are then perfectly flat.   If you line it make single seams and press them open before sewing in the lining.

The square-necked bodice (page 192) fastens in the front with small beads and buttonhole loops.   If you use felt, buttonhole slits can be cut in the front.   The decoration is a border of pinked felt in a contrasting colour with short fly stitch branches round the waistline and a long one coming from the shoulder.

The last waistcoat is shorter than the others.   It does not reach to the waistline. The fastening consists of a lacing made from a narrow twisted cord threaded through evenly matched buttonhole loops attached to each of the fronts.   Make sure your cord is long enough to tie in a bow.   Finish the ends with small tassels.

DRESS BODICES

I have included (page 194) a bodice pattern for a dress.   The sleeve can be taken from the blouse section and the skirt is a matter of taste, flared, gathered, pleated, etc. The dress bodice is taken from the inside lines on the diagram.   Make it exactly as for

Waistcoat and bolero

191

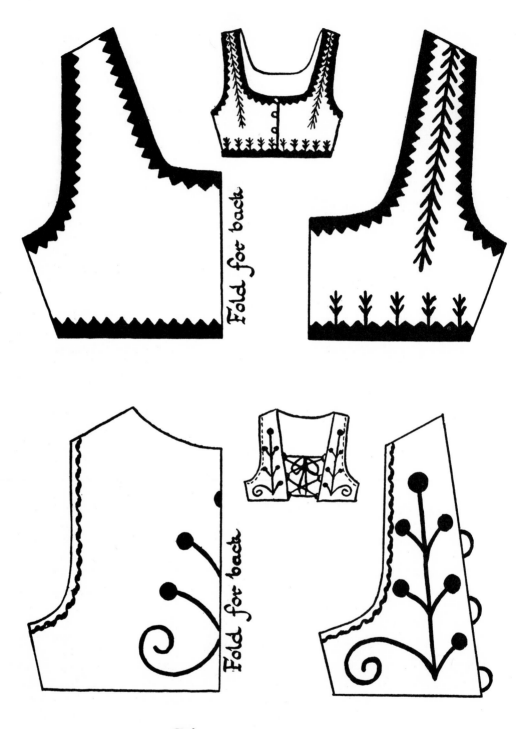

Two bodices

the blouse, with the addition of darts, which are sewn in on the wrong side. The original is fastened down the back. It is in a fine stripe with a gathered skirt, the back opening of which meets the back opening of the bodice. The neck is bound with a crossway strip but any one of the collars would look very well. If you do use a collar pattern remember to have it in two halves because of the back opening. The sleeve is the puff sleeve pattern. Many different ways of using stripes, spots, checks, etc., will no doubt occur to you when you come to make the dress.

The second dress is a pinafore style which is worn over a blouse. Back and front bodices are alike, each cut from double material. Join the two back pieces to the front pieces across the shoulders—single seams; then join both lengths together down the sides —all on the wrong side. Turn to the right side and fold in the turnings round the neck. Seam along this edge neatly.

Now make a gathered skirt on a band. Sew the bodice to the inside of the skirt band, having the placket opening at the side. Decorative running stitch round the bodice and along the hem finishes off the pinafore dress.

NIGHTDRESS

For the nightdress there is a round yoke. Blouses or dresses can also be made from this same pattern. The fastening is at the back and the yoke is double, so cut two front sections with a fold in the centre and four back sections—two for each side. Sew two back pieces to a front piece along the shoulders with a single seam. Repeat this with the second set of shapes.

Cut the long skirt sections—back and front alike with a fold down the centre. Cut them to the length required, remembering to leave room for a frill if you wish it. Join down the sides with a French seam, and across the tiny straight shoulder section with a single seam on the wrong side. Cut a slit down the centre back and hem it on to the wrong side, tapering it towards the bottom and oversewing the end of the slit to prevent fraying. Then gather along the top curved edges between the marks on the pattern. Pull up the gathers until they fit the lower edge of the yoke. Backstitch the two sections together on the wrong side, remembering to turn in the straight edges of the back yoke. The shoulder line of the skirt will stand out a little but this is taken in when the sleeves are added. Now sew the second yoke section to the first along the neck edge on the wrong side. Clip the curved edge and turn on to the right side. Fold under the raw edges and hem the lower curved edge on to the gathers. Seam along the straight sides of the back yoke opening. All the raw edges are enclosed.

Make the sleeves from the blouse pattern, using the fullest sleeve set into a cuff. Sew these into the armholes so that the sleeve seam exactly meets the yoke seam on the shoulder. Trim the seam on the inside and bind with a narrow crossway strip.

A frill may be added to the lower hem. Cut a length of fabric about one and a half times as long as the distance round the hem and join it with a run and fell. Turn under the bottom hem of the frill and stitch it down. Turn down a hem along the top edge of the frill and run a gathering thread round, taking care to see that it fastens the hem down as well.

Then lay a hem along the bottom edge of the nightdress. Pull the gathers so that

Pinafore dress
bodice

Line for dress bodice

Place to fold for centre front of dress

Fold for centre back of coat

Nightdress bodice

Nightdress yoke

Fold for centre front

Fold

Patterns for nightdress
and dress bodices

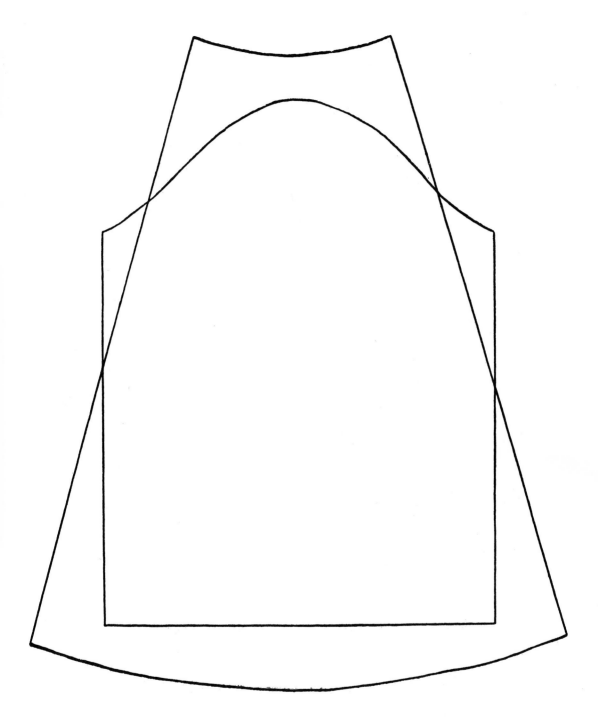

Coat sleeve and skirt patterns

they fit the nightdress and carefully tack the frill on to the nightdress hem, catching it down as you go along.   Then machine or hand sew it over the gathering thread.   If it is in the correct position you will sew the nightdress hem down at the same time.   A little embroidery worked on the yoke, cuffs and hem looks attractive.   Fasten the back opening with hooks and bars down the yoke, or loops and very tiny hand-made buttons—a very small circle of cloth stuffed with cotton wool.

COAT

The dress bodice—the larger size—is suitable for a coat.   Use the round blouse collar.   Make all the seams single and press them open on the wrong side.

The skirt (page 195) is in four sections.   Join them and then stitch to the bodice. Join the sleeve seams and fit into the armhole.   Any extra fullness can be pleated into a box pleat on top of the sleeve.   Make a lining without the sleeves.   Stitch the lining round the armholes without any turning.   Turn in the fronts and bottom hems of both coat and lining and slip stitch together.

Make the sleeve lining.   Fit it inside the sleeve and turn a hem round the top edge, sewing it over the raw edge of the armhole.   Turn under both lining and cuff edge and slip stitch together.   Cut a collar from outer fabric and lining, stitching them together round the curved edge on the wrong side.   Sew the collar on to the coat, leaving a space at each front for overlapping.   If you add fur trimming choose one which is short and neat.

APRONS

The aprons (page 197) are very simple in construction.   Most are rectangles gathered into bands just like the gathered skirts.   The bibs are added next, stitched to the back of the waistbands.   If you use checks or other patterns keep them small in scale.   The same applies to any other decoration whether it is embroidery, braid or lace trimming.

BRACES, BELTS AND POCKETS

Felt is good for braces, belts and pockets (diagrams on page 198).   Then the pockets need not be lined.   The belts and braces, however, are better lined even if the outside is felt.   A fine cotton lining is suitable.   If you make the pockets from fabric which frays, remember to add turnings to the pattern and cut each section twice.   Then turn in the edges after working the embroidery, and seam them together.   Use fishbone stitch for joining the shoulders of felt braces.   These are sewn on to a belt.   A slit in the felt serves as a buttonhole with a large bead for a button.   On other fabrics you must of course work buttonhole stitch round the opening.   Trousers for boy dolls, golliwogs or clowns can be adapted from the knicker pattern.

HATS AND BONNETS

Some of the hat shapes may have to be adapted.   They all depend on the amount of hair you have given your doll, and its style.   Try the shapes in paper first, making them larger or smaller if necessary.   Straight pins with glass bead heads are useful for hatpins.

First there are two bonnet patterns (page 199).   One has a straight piece from the

Some dolls' aprons

Pocket

Belts, braces and
pockets

Shapes for two bonnets

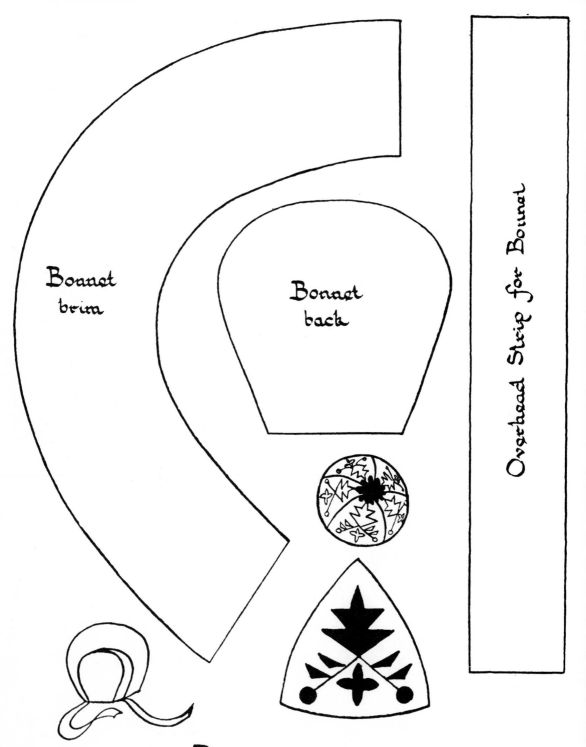

Bonnet
brim

Bonnet
back

Overhead Strip for Bonnet

Poke bonnet and cap

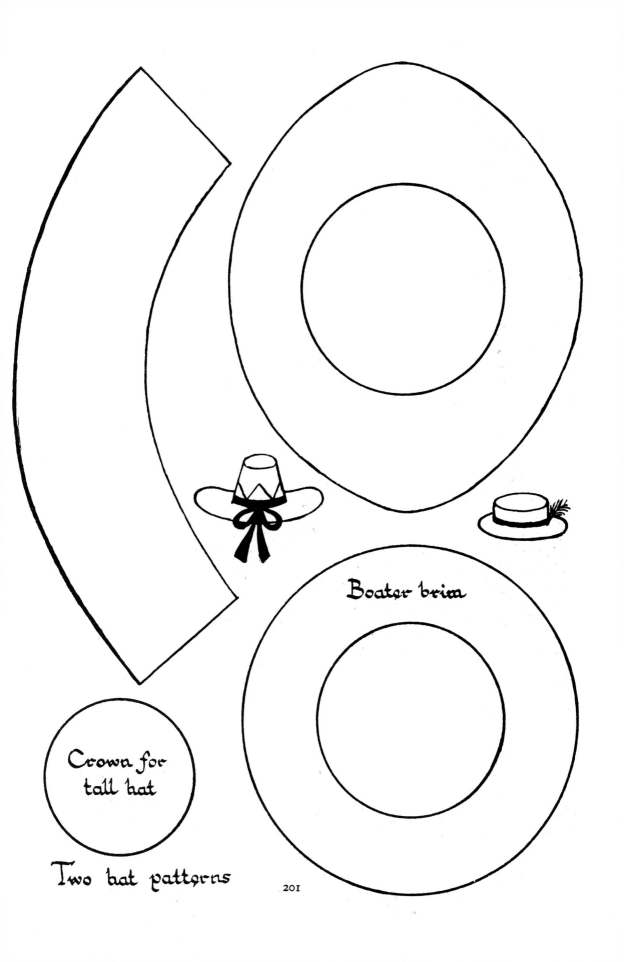

Boater brim

Crown for
tall hat

Two hat patterns

201

front of the head to the back of the neck with two side pieces stitched to it.   Once again felt is good for these shapes.   Work the embroidery before assembling the pieces.   If you use other fabric leave small turnings which go to the inside of the hat.

The second bonnet has a single piece for the back with a long, shaped strip which goes over the head.   Both bonnets are better lined with some thin fabric.

Then we have a poke bonnet (page 200) built up from the previous shape; a single piece for the back with a straight strip stitched round it going over the head, then the curved brim sewn on to that.   The brim is firmer with tailor's canvas or even thin pliable card stitched between double material.   A felt outside with a silk lining—perhaps ruched —would be attractive.   Keep fur or braid trimmings in proportion with the bonnet and do not forget to line the crown also.

The small skull cap fits on the back of the head.   It consists of five sections sewn together.   Line this too and finish the centre with a pom-pom or tassel.

The next two patterns (page 201) are for hats with crowns.   The boater is simple to construct.   It comprises two circles of felt with a round hole in the middle of each. One of the circles cut from the brim will serve as the top of the crown.   You will also need a straight strip of felt long enough to fit round this circle.   Join the two ends of the strip together and then sew it to the crown.   Sew the outer edges of the two large circles together.   Now sew the lower edge of the straight piece to the inside circle of the brim. The double felt of the brim keeps it fairly rigid.   You can decorate the hat with ribbons, cords, feathers, bows, fruit or flowers.

The second hat has a higher tapering crown.   Sew the curved section together along the straight edges, using fishbone stitch.   Then fit in the small circular crown.   Cut two brim pieces and sew them together round the outer edges.   Sometimes it is a good plan to have the hat in two colours.   (If you wish to bend the brim about sew in a piece of fine wire when you are fixing the two brims.)   Then stitch the crown into the brim. You can make very charming raffia hats in the way described for making baskets on the donkey earlier in the book.   Be certain to keep the raffia fine and the stitching small so that the hats will not be clumsy or bulky.

FOOTWEAR

Finally we come to footwear.   All the shoes and boots on pages 203–4 with the exception of the moccasins have the same sole pattern.   It is advisable to cut this in paper first, and test it for size on your doll's foot.   A stiff sole has two layers of fabric with a piece of card between.   Felt, leather, american cloth or anything that does not fray is suitable for shoes.   A shoe with a stiff sole is more difficult to take off.

The first pattern is a simple slipper enriched with decorative stitching.   Sew the backs together with fishbone and then sew the uppers to the soles.   Further stitching or couching may be added round the sole.

The tie shoe is based on the same pattern.   The tiny round holes are cut with a leather-punch.   Use a fine twisted cord for the tie with bobbles or tassels on the ends.

A third variation is the ankle strap.   Make it in the same way as the slipper with the addition of a narrow strip sewn to the back of the shoe.   This should be long enough to come round the ankle.   Fasten at the front with a buttonhole and bead.

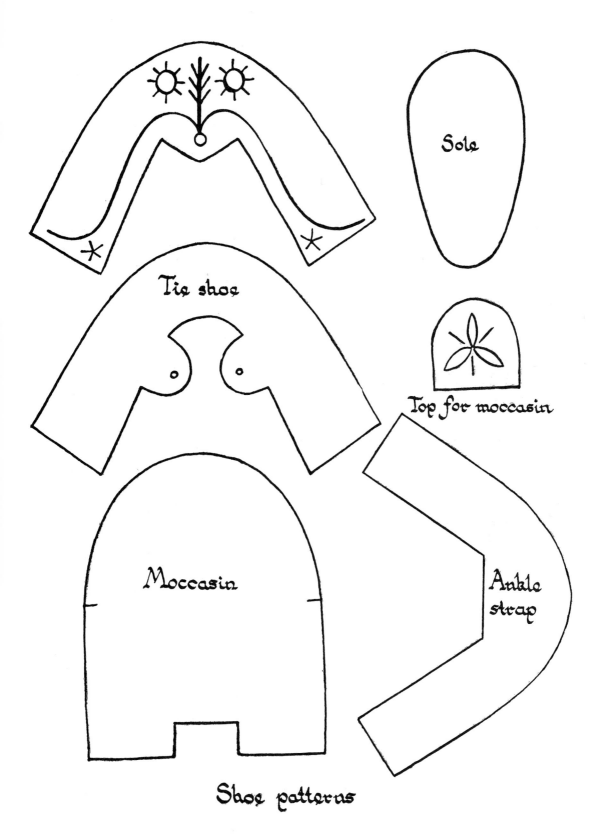

Sole

Tie shoe

Top for moccasin

Moccasin

Ankle strap

Shoe patterns

203

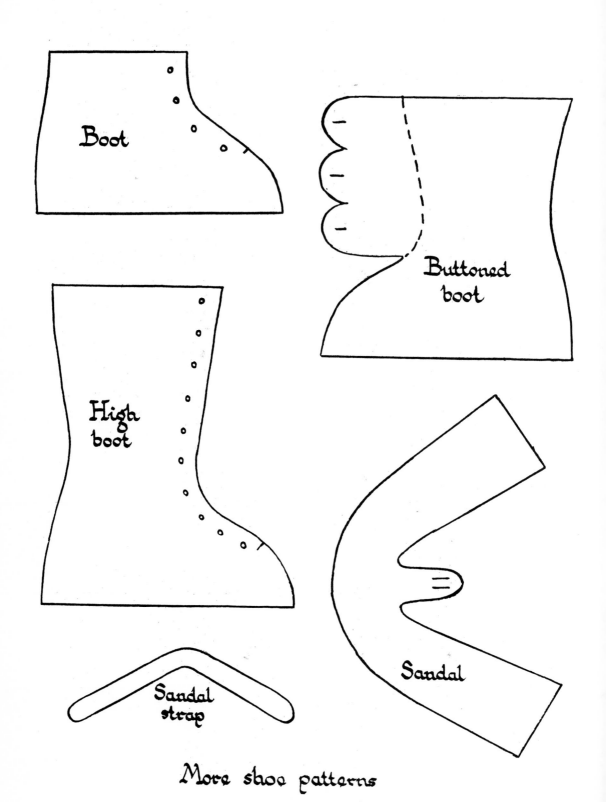

Boot

Buttoned
boot

High
boot

Sandal

Sandal
strap

More shoe patterns

The sandal is similar in type. The bar this time is slightly shaped and attached to the inside of the shoe. It slips through two slits in the tongue and fastens with buttonhole and bead on the outside. Try the strap for position before finally sewing it.

The moccasin consists of a shape which forms the sole and sides all in one with a small piece for the top of the foot. Sew the two straight back edges together. Then sew along the bottom of the heel. Gather round the curved edge between the marks and pull up the gathers so that they fit round the curved part of the small front section. Oversew these pieces together. Try to sew in between each gather so that the stitching appears even.

The long and short boots are alike in construction. Each boot consists of two pieces sewn down the back and a little way up the front—as far as the mark on the pattern. Make very small holes and lace the boots up to the top. The high boots look quite well with the tops turned down a little way.

For the Victorian button boot each one has one half cut to the dotted line on the pattern and the other cut with the scalloped overlap. Sew them together down the back and along the front as far as the beginning of the overlap. The scalloped half is on the inside of the foot so that it can wrap round and fasten on the outside. Each boot of course is sewn on to a sole. Cut slits for the buttonholes and sew on beads for the buttons.

You may wish to make thicker soles. If so, cut layers of card and cover them with felt or leather. A wedge heel is made by having extra card in the sole. Start with the full sole, then add a piece which only reaches to the instep. Continue adding shorter pieces of card until the heel is built to the desired depth. Cover the whole thing with a second complete sole and fold a strip of felt or leather right round the edge. Next stitch on an upper and under sole covering the raw edges of the piece which is folded round the outside.

CRADLE

Someone might like to make a family of dolls using the different sizes. For example, mother, elder daughter, younger daughter and baby. So page 206 shows a simple pattern for a cradle. It is assembled like the donkey cart described earlier in the book (page 115). Cut two pieces of felt for each end—two contrasting colours—and a piece of card to go in between them. Work your design and then seam the felts together round the card. Make the body of the cradle from a piece of card 5″ square covered on each side with felt. Choose firm but flexible card. Sew the body sections to the sloping sides of the end piece, letting the middle of the body section curve round to form the base of the cradle. The seams may be covered with a couched thread or a twisted or knotted cord.

TO END WITH

For conclusion I would just like to emphasize that these patterns are only suggestions to encourage those who are perhaps a little afraid of drawing their own designs, and making their own shapes. Once you have started I am quite certain that any number of ideas and adaptations will occur to you, and that you will derive a great enjoyment and delight from creating toys to your individual requirements.

Dolls' cradles

INDEX